Realistic Plastic Structures for Toy Train Layouts

Art Curren

KALMBACH BOOKS

© 1998 Art Curren. All rights reserved. This book may not be reproduced in part or in whole without written permission of the publisher, except in the case of brief quotations used in reviews. Published by Kalmbach Publishing Co., 21027 Crossroads Circle, Waukesha, WI 53187.

Printed in the United States of America

97 98 99 00 01 02 03 04 05 06   10 9 8 7 6 5 4 3 2 1

For more information, visit our website at http://www.kalmbach.com

Publisher's Cataloging-in-Publication
(Provided by Quality Books, Inc.)

Curren, Art.
 Realistic plastic structures for toy train layouts / Art Curren. — 1st ed.
 p. cm.
 ISBN 0-89778-410-3

 1. Railroads—Models.   I. Title.

TF197.C87 1997   625.1'9
                            QBI97-1525

Book design: Mark Watson
Cover design: Kristi Ludwig

CONTENTS

Introduction to Kitbashing 5
    Practical Doodling 9

1   **The Tipakull Factory** 12

2   **A Small Brick Depot** 21

3   **A Block of Stores** 29

4   **Three Rico Stations** 41
    Warning: Kit in box 54

5   **A Yard Office and an Elevated Grade Crossing Shanty** 55

6   **Bigg Industries** 60

7   **Term Oil Company** 63

8   **Nopeeks Variety Store** 68

9   **Kold Coal Company** 72

Appendix A: Signs 79

Appendix B: Suppliers and Manufacturers 80

DEDICATION

This book is dedicated to my father, Arthur E. Curren, a fellow author.

You will learn how easy it is to make unique structures, such as this one, from the pages of this book.

Introduction to Kitbashing

Welcome to a new experience, kitbashing. Kitbashing may be both a new experience in modeling and a new word. A softer version of this word might be kitmingling. In either case these words describe modifying a kit, or kits, in some way. Often it is a minor change, but at other times the modification may be a major departure from what the kit's manufacturer had in mind. Kitmingling, which can also apply to combining kits or partial kits without actually modifying the parts much, doesn't have to involve structures. You can also kitmingle rolling stock and locomotives. For instance, you can cut both a baggage car and a coach in half and put them back together as a combine. (If you are careful, you might be able to get two combines out if it!) Kitmingling lets you achieve a different look for a building or anything else, giving your layout some distinctive features rather than having every building look like thousands of others. (If you get some of the ideas from this book, I won't tell anyone.)

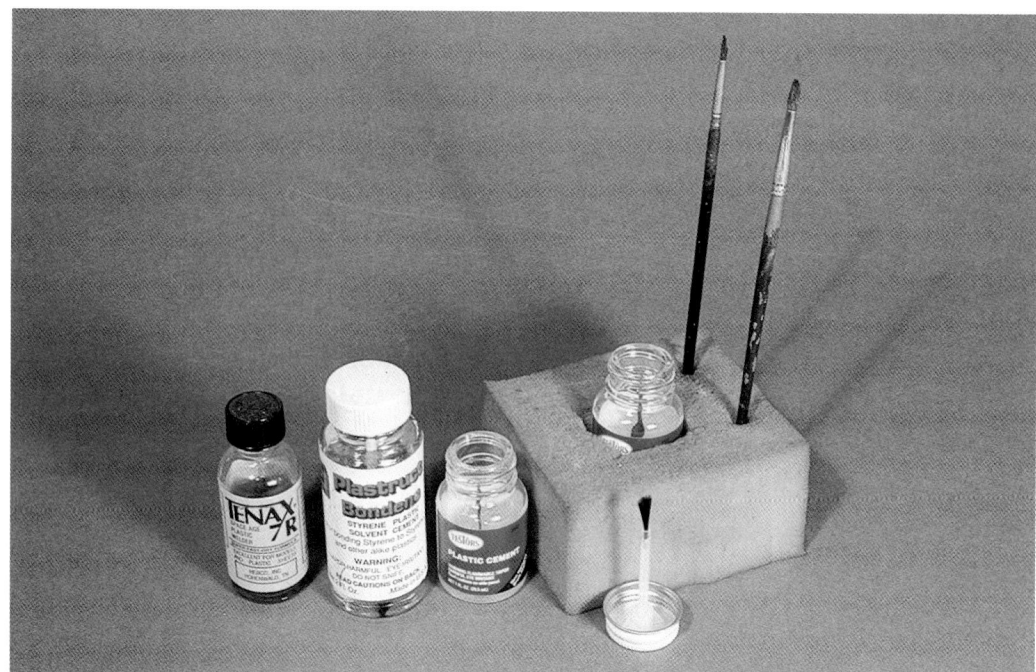

Fig. 1. The most popular bonding solvent is Testor's, which I prefer to other brands. To prevent spillage, make a holder like this one from a piece of foam cushion. The hole in it holds the solvent bottle and a pair of small brushes, a no. 2 and a no. 5.

A FRAME OF MIND

I have often heard, "If a manufacturer has gone to such great pains to design and produce a kit, how dare you have the audacity to alter it!" Many collectors will be appalled at altering a kit, saying that it diminishes the kit's value. As good as a kit may be, it may not be exactly what I had in mind for my situation. Thus, that kit has no value to me, other than providing me with parts to make something that will better fit my needs than a "stock kit" would. It's my option to make a few changes and adapt it to my needs.

As a technique, kitmingling gives you greater freedom than any other technique I know. If you use some of the principles in this book, you will be able to make many special buildings using readily available kits as the basic materials and taking them one, two, or many steps beyond what the manufacturer intended. What you achieve will depend on the degree of effort and desire you put into it.

THE TWO COMMANDMENTS

There are two rules that will get you through any project. First, don't ever consider that what the manufacturer calls a "kit" is all that the parts in the kit can ever add up to be. Second, don't be afraid to make the first cut on a kit. Master these two simple rules and you can make almost anything you might need.

I will show you many different techniques for making your buildings look unique and more realistic. Some will be repeated, but most will be new.

BUILDING CHOICES

I have chosen to make a lot of industrial buildings in this book simply because there are far fewer of them on the market than there are houses and town buildings. In most cases I have made a larger structure out of smaller ones. The techniques can be applied to any size or kind of building. In many cases you can make some of the simpler changes rather than the more complex ones described. You can use as much or as little of the information as you want to achieve goals that you set for yourself. After a few kitmingling projects, you will soon arrive at a "comfort zone" that suits your style of modeling. As your confidence grows, you will become more daring in your kitmingling attempts.

SUPPLIES

For each building project, you will find a list of different sizes or kinds of sheet, strip, and tube styrene that I used to modify or replace parts of a kit. I use styrene made by Evergreen Scale Models and Plastruct, the major suppliers of many styrene items. I use lots of different sizes, and you will need to get a supply from the hobby shop. By the time you finish this book, you will have a good supply that you can use for many future projects.

SOME GLUE BASICS

Since all of the kits in this book are made from some form of styrene plastic, it is appropriate to take a look at working with this material. Styrene has many different properties. It can be cut and bonded easily, it takes paint well, and manufacturers can mold exquisite detail into its surface. Some of the kits are advertised as "snap fit," requiring no glue for assembly. This is technically true, but these kits are prone to fall apart if you look at them sideways. It is better to bond, not glue, them together. The liquid solvent used to bond styrene together actually melts or softens the top surface of the plastic. When you place two pieces against one another, they weld together as the solvent evaporates. You can proceed very rapidly since there is no need to wait for glue to set up or dry.

There are different kinds of solvents. The slow evaporation of Testor's is preferable to the fast evaporation of Tenax, which is not good for fastening large joints. Tenax is good for joining tiny parts that might be dissolved by the slower evaporating Testor's. Bondine and Ambroid are other brands that evaporate at a rate between that of Testor's and Tenax. There are thick solvents in a tube that you should avoid altogether. They contain fillers, take forever to set up, and produce a poor bond. They can also be very messy.

I use plenty of solvent rather than worry about it running where it is not wanted. Contrary to what some other modelers tell you, if you use too little solvent, it evaporates before the plastic has sufficiently melted the two surfaces and bonding does not occur. Oozing plastic at the joints tells you the joint will be solid. Wait until the oozing plastic solidifies and shave it off with a chisel blade. If you get any solvent on a detailed surface, don't touch it; wait until it dries. It will never be seen.

TOOLS AND CUTTING

Cutting styrene is also easy. First use a knife fitted with a no. 11 blade to scribe a groove in the plastic. If the plastic is thick, use a razor saw to finish the cut. On thinner plastic keep on with the knife until the cut is all the way through. Do not cut with the sharp edge of the blade; use the opposite edge instead. This slices a sliver of plastic out of the groove. The sharp edge just pushes the plastic out of the way, creating two raised areas on each side of the cut, which takes longer to get through.

To cut Evergreen styrene, scribe a line and snap it apart at that line, just like using a glass cutter. Do not try this snapping method on a molded kit wall. It may shatter or tear, leaving a ragged edge. During the casting of the hot molten styrene, stresses are built up within the wall. It will snap at the weakest point, usually not where you want it to snap. Some styrenes are rubbery and some are brittle (the majority are somewhere in between). Styrenes of both extremes are the worst as far as cutting and snapping is concerned. To eliminate problems, don't take a chance by snapping.

OTHER TOOLS

Besides the razor saw, the other tools that are must-haves are a steel straightedge, tweezers, and some files. Drills, a pin vise, pliers, cutters, and other tweezers and saws also come in handy, as does a brass bristle suede shoe brush for knocking off the "fuzzie-wuzzies" that filing and cutting produce. Other knife handles and blades, such as chisel blades, are useful in some situations. I have many handles, each with a different blade, as well as pin vises. I have a different drill size in four of them. It is easier to reach for the correct knife or drill than having to change them all the time. After a while you will accumulate a lot of convenient tools that make the job easier.

A battery-operated Dremel drill at slow speed is good for plastic use (high speeds cause too much heat and melt the plastic). Some people use a hot knife to cut plastic, but I never had any luck with it. A hot knife is good for rough cutting, since it leaves a ragged edge, and for starting an opening in the center of a piece. Try using one and see how it does for you.

A copier is one tool that will not fit in your toolbox. Use it to copy the kit walls and roofs and use the copies to determine how and where you might cut or modify a part to achieve what you want. Lacking access to a copier, you can trace the kit parts onto paper and do the same thing, allowing you to see your results without

Fig. 2. To the left of the ruler are the basic tools. The ones to the right are extras that are handy to have and make many jobs easier.

actually cutting any kit parts. This is a great way to plan what you want to accomplish and find out if it is achievable.

WEATHERING

To look realistic, an item has to give the impression that it has been around a while. This is especially true of something that was built fifty or more years ago. For something to look old, it has to show the ravages of time and the effect nature has had on it over its life span. Bleached paint, rotting wood, dirt accumulation, and even a few broken or repaired parts all signify that this item has been standing in its place for quite a while.

There are a few ways to simulate this natural occurrence. The first would be to remove the shine of the plastic from which the kit is made. A coat of Testor's Dullcote spray lacquer will achieve this easily. Even a freshly painted building will begin to dull down in only a few months. Years will take an even heavier toll. (See Chapter 9 for more information on an easy technique for weathering.)

PAINTING

For the most part, I rely on Floquil brand paint. Here is where I will contradict most modelers who suggest using Floquil on plastic. Floquil is a lacquer-based paint and the solvent in it (Diosol) can even be used as a bonding agent, so it does react with plastic. However, unless you puddle a whole lot of paint in one area, you can brush-paint if you paint rapidly and do not scrub or leave thick coats in one spot. Airbrushing is another way to apply Floquil directly on plastic with no ill effects. If you are still timid, Floquil does have a coat called Barrier that you can brush on first and then paint over with regular Floquil. Floquil also makes a line of paints designed for plastics and there are other brands of water-based or enamel paints you can substitute if you choose. Just be sure to use flat paints rather than glossy. All of these products should be available in most well-stocked hobby shops.

CONCLUSION

The chapters that follow use the basic information you've just read and add a few new things to help you along. Since I mention some procedures only once, it may be wise to read the whole book to learn them even if the only building you decide to make is in one of the last chapters.

Last, in addition to the two commandments I mentioned earlier, I would like to add a very important third one: Read and heed the instructions that come in each kit. This will familiarize you with the parts in the kit and how they are to be assembled. As we journey through this book, I will often expand upon each kit's directions, and that's what kitmingling is all about.

PRACTICAL DOODLING

Almost everyone doodles once in a while. Although usually just a bunch of nonsense, doodling can have practical results. The doodling examples shown here illustrate two of the basic approaches I use in my kitmingling. The first approach is to have a kit in front of me and then see what I might be able to make from it. The second is to have a definite goal in mind and then set out to find what kit or parts I need to achieve that goal.

As you can see, a doodle doesn't have to be a great work of art. It is just a tool you can use to see if something may work. Doodling is also an easy way to check and make sure if you have enough pieces to continue with a project, abandon it, or modify it from your original plan.

DOODLE IDEA NUMBER 1

This doodle (fig. 3) illustrates my first approach. I saw an ad for a series of town buildings made by Buildings Unlimited. I had seen many of these buildings in layout photos, so I knew what all four walls looked like. This meant I could make my doodle without actually owning the kit. If I had not known what the walls looked like, I could have bought the kit and then proceeded to examine what building I might make from these parts.

I thought that if I bought one extra rear wall (the different walls are available separately), I could make an addition that would change the look considerably. This would fulfill another kitmingling criterion, that of creating a unique structure. This series of buildings is designed with kitmingling in mind; the back of the walls is conveniently scored halfway through, so cutting them apart is easy. It is a good idea, though, to make copies of the wall pieces before cutting or modifying them; then you can use the copies to figure out where the walls should be cut.

To make a large factory with these kits, take two of them and double the width and length, making a boxlike building. This quadruples the original 6" x 6" area to 12" x 12". This is the doodle shown in fig. 4.

Using the same two kits, I doodled some more and came up with a unique building that has an even larger footprint and a more interesting shape (fig. 5). There are endless possibilities beyond these doodles! The more you doodle, the more you will see how easy it is to design a building to fit your space.

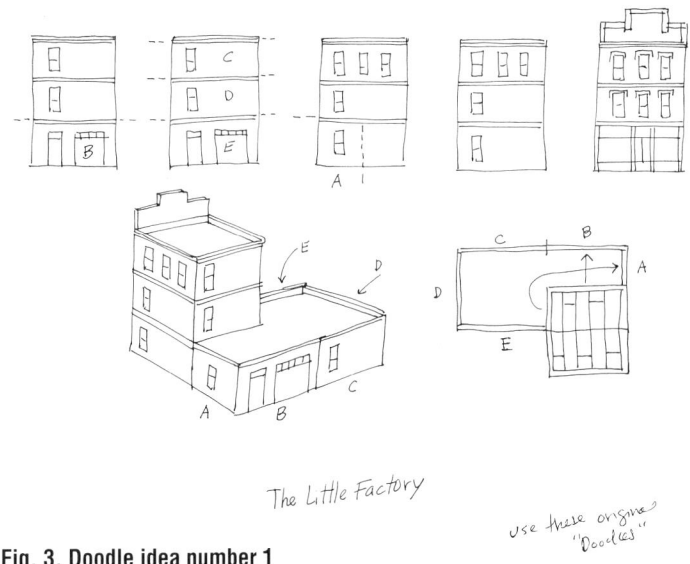

Fig. 3. Doodle idea number 1

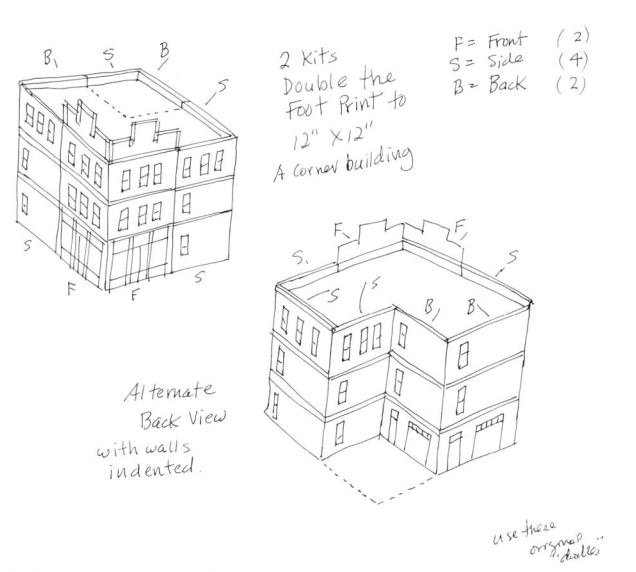

Fig. 4. Doodle idea number 1 doubled

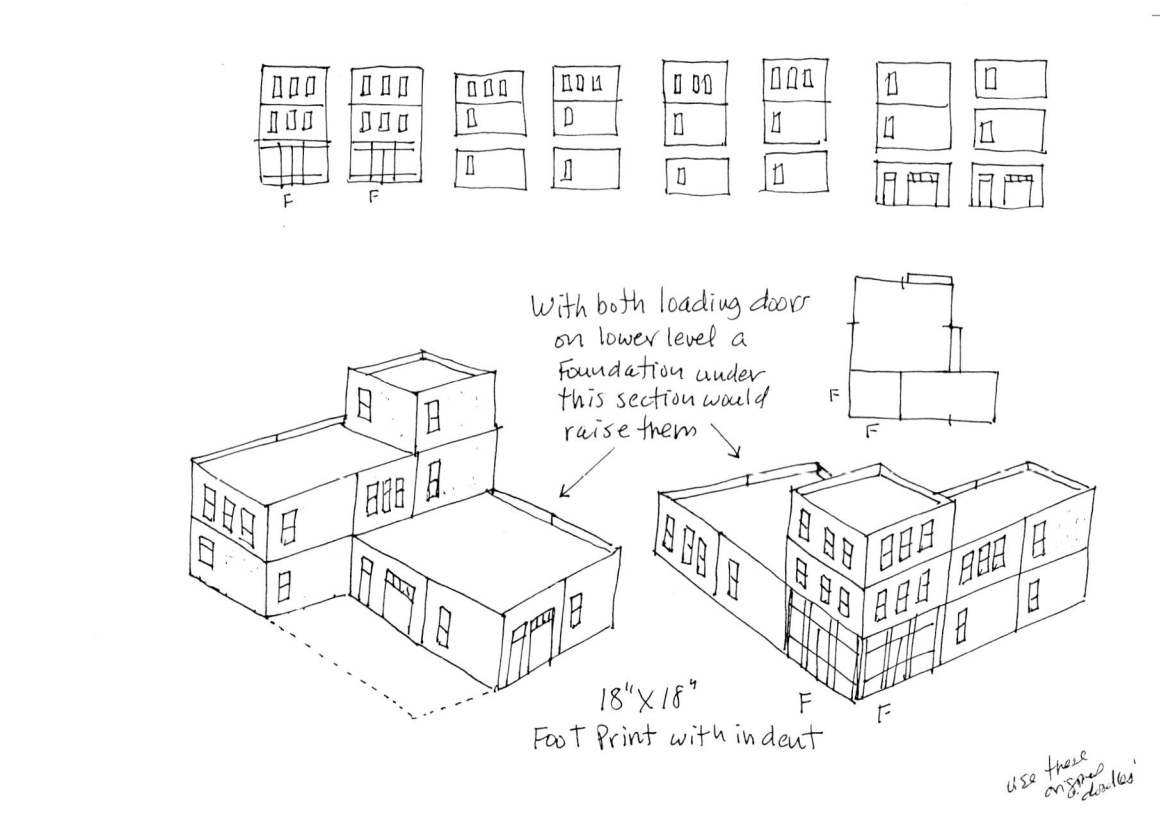

Fig. 5. Doodle idea number 1 expanded

DOODLE IDEA NUMBER 2

This doodle illustrates my second approach. I wanted to make a typical small brick depot, which is not available on the market. I chose to use Design Preservation Models' series of modular brick wall sections, which come in a variety of door and window configurations. The DPM catalog shows small drawings of all the available walls, so I made a doodle using these as a guide. The doodle shows how I might combine some of these wall sections to make the brick depot. I wanted to include an operator's bay window in front of the depot, so I doodled how I might cut up a three-window wall to get the bay sides and a two-window wall to make the front of the bay and to fill in an equal space in the rear wall. I thought I could cut two triangular sections from the blank brick wall to make peaks for the end walls.

Once I finished the doodles, I used the planning packet drawings that DPM sells separately to check and see if my doodle was, indeed, workable. It was (fig. 6).

Fig. 6. Doodle idea number 2

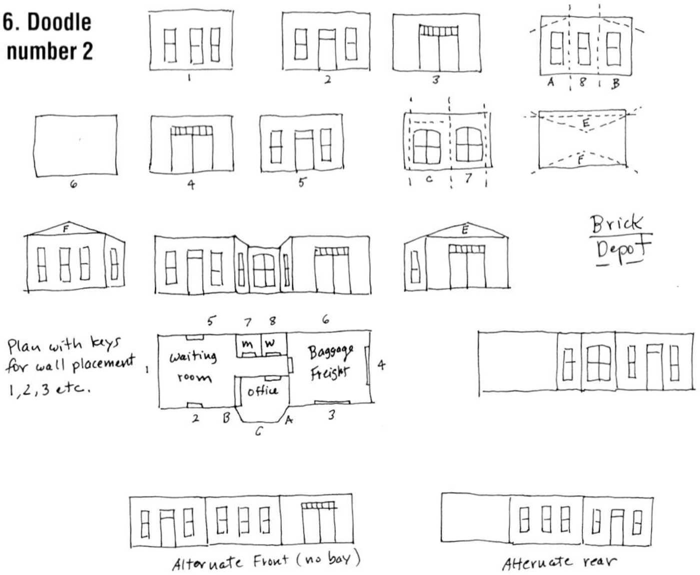

DOODLE IDEA NUMBER 3

The third doodle embraces both approaches. Here I wanted a city block. I started with the two new Walthers O scale Cornerstone Series kits and the extra parts each kit provides. These kits use

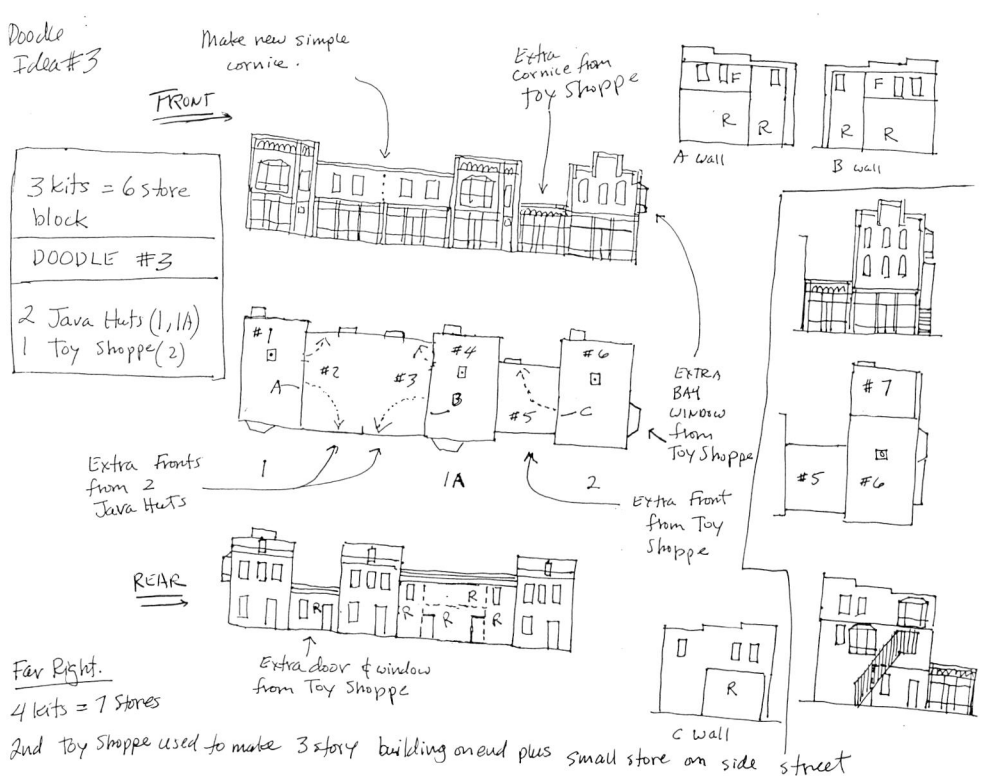

Fig. 7. Doodle idea number 3

common roof, base, chimney, and side and rear wall parts, but the front walls differ in each kit. In addition both kits include three sprues that have common parts so you won't need some if you are only making one building. Rather than let these go to waste, I doodled a way to make seven storefronts out of three kits. (Now, I call that "practical.") The dotted lines indicate how I might cut and fold some of the side walls (A, B, C, and D) to make new front and back walls for the four new stores.

Taking this thought one step farther, I doodled what the Toy Shoppe might look like if I used a second kit to make an additional story. I also added an outside covered stairway to reach the second story and used up the two extra bay windows. This additional modification just demonstrates how many ideas you can concoct with a doodle (fig. 7).

MAKING DOODLES A REALITY

In the following three chapters you will see how I turned a few of these basic doodles into actual buildings.

It is easy to find room for a small factory on your layout, and it makes a busy scene when goods are ready to be shipped to customers.

1 The Tipakull Factory

The Tipakull Manufacturing Co. is the first of my doodles come to life. It is also an example of turning a city business building into a revenue producer for the railroad. This factory could be part of a city block of buildings that just happen to have a track running behind them, which is a typical scene in some small cities. If built as a three-story building without the addition, it would seem rather small to have a loading dock on the siding track. Through the magic of kitmingling, though, I gave it a larger footprint that should be just enough to warrant having a boxcar deliver goods once or twice a week.

THE BASIC PREMISE

Remember from the "Practical Doodling" sidebar in the Introduction that I wanted to enlarge this building with a minimal amount of work to make the footprint more than double the original. As a matter of fact, this one is so simple that we can use the doodle as our instructions. I will also show you a few techniques that will be used many times throughout this book.

The kit I used is one of a series of six city buildings made by Buildings Unlimited. They are just about the simplest kits on the market with four walls, a roof (a cornice in some cases), and a piece of sidewalk. Each has a different front and all share the same sides and rear walls, so from the front they all look different, but from the sides or rear, they all look alike. I used kit no. 872, Bill's Store. Fortunately, you can buy walls separately, so I purchased an extra no. 70 rear wall.

HOW TO CUT

These kits have a wonderful feature not often found on plastic kits: they provide score marks across the inside at each floor level so they can be cut easily at these points. (They were obviously designed with kitmingling in mind.) I say "cut" because the instructions tell you to snap the pieces over a table edge. Do not do this unless you want a ragged edge that may be hard to clean up and make right. Instead, partially scribe the fronts with a knife just above the raised row of vertical bricks, as shown in fig. 1-1. Scribing here matches where the groove is on the back. You do not even need a rule to scribe here because the raised vertical row of bricks will guide the knife. Next, saw the rest of the way through the walls. The score marks on the back are deep, and the scribing on the front leaves only a thin section of plastic wall that is fairly easy to saw through.

WHERE TO CUT

My doodle shows that I wanted to cut one rear wall on the lowest score mark to remove the first floor. I cut the extra rear wall at both score marks, creating three wall sections each one floor high. Actually the top of the top floor had a tile capping that made it a little taller. I removed this. Since there was no score mark on the back at this location, this was a harder cut to make because I was sawing through the full thickness of the wall. In addition to the 3/16"-thick wall, there was a raised

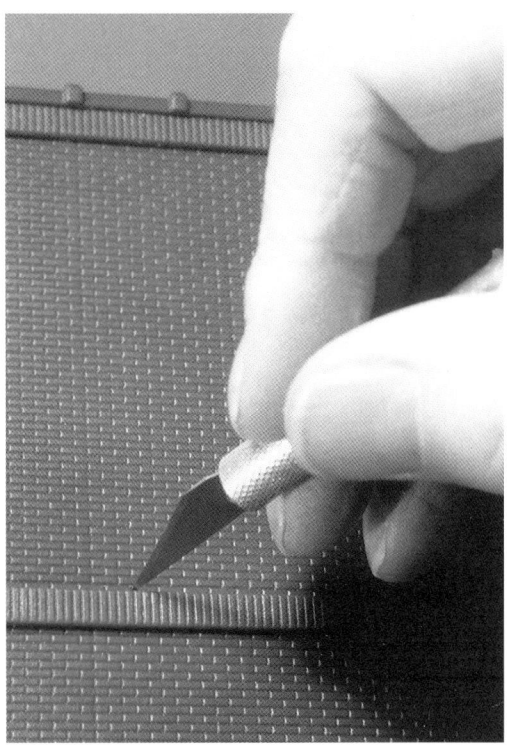

Fig. 1-1. I cut the walls along the upper edge of the raised row of vertical bricks that separate each floor.

Fig. 1-2. Here are the walls showing where I cut them apart. The lower floor is separated from the extra rear wall. The three floors are separated from the other rear wall, and the tile cap has been removed. The lower half has been removed from the side wall.

course of vertical bricks that increased the thickness to 1/4". I took my time scribing and sawing this.

One of the side walls also needed cutting, and I cut this one through the lower score mark to the middle of the wall. Then I sawed vertically up from the bottom to meet the first saw cut. This removed just half of the bottom wall section on this side

Fig. 1-3. Here the walls are assembled into the two units.

wall. Fig. 1-2 shows how all the walls looked after the cutting was done.

WHERE TO PUT THE NEW WALLS

After filing all of the cut edges smooth, you can begin assembling the main part of the building. I started by adding the tile capping, which I had removed from the top of the rear wall, to the top of the front wall. You can use the fancy cornice as intended, if you wish, but I wanted a plainer look, so I used the tile instead.

At this point, my front wall and one side wall were intact and the other walls had both upper floors. One had a partial lower floor. I bonded this unit together. There are guides on the inside of the front and back walls to aid in placing the side walls against the front and back walls correctly. I used them and added more bracing made from 1/8" square strip, which I usually do. To ensure the building was square, I inserted the roof in place but did not bond it. I used rubber bands around the building to help hold it together while the solvent set in the joints. I then let this set up solidly overnight.

THE ADDITION

Once the basic structure is set, it is time to add the addition, which is what makes this building exclusive. You now have a few options. Before cutting the half wall from the one side, you should choose on which side you want to place the addition. If you are placing it on the side opposite to where I placed mine, cut away the opposite section from the lower side wall. If you're more timid, cut up only the extra wall and add it to either of the sides or to the back against a completely uncut original Bill's Store. If you go this way, you will only double the footprint, since the addition will only go in one direction (mine goes both back and to the side, so the footprint is larger). The third option is to raise the addition by adding a foundation beneath it to bring it up to the height of the loading dock. This is a bit tricky, because

Fig. 1-4. Without a foundation, the building would look like this.

the addition's roof can't rise above the bottoms of the windows on the second floor.

Now, to assemble the addition. (If you go with placing the addition on the side opposite to mine, the installation procedures are identical.) At any point where the cut sections of the rear wall meet something else, you must file or saw off the side edge of the raised nub of the vertical brick strip at the top of each segment. You should think this out carefully.

To make things easier, I filed off the raised nub from the half section. I bonded this to the lower portion that I had removed from the main rear wall, which had actually been pushed straight back. This is the section with the two doors. Then, after filing off both nubs where these join, I bonded the cut-off middle section next to that. I added scrap plastic braces across this butt joint for additional strength. I then added the cut-off top section at right angles to that. Both nubs are filed off this wall. Last, at right angles I added the lower cut-off section with the doors. I only filed off the nub toward the main wall. Now, if I hadn't intended to add a foundation, I could have attached this addition to the assembled main building (see figs. 1-3 and 1-4).

THE FOUNDATIONS

I did want to raise the addition, so I added the foundation by cutting strips

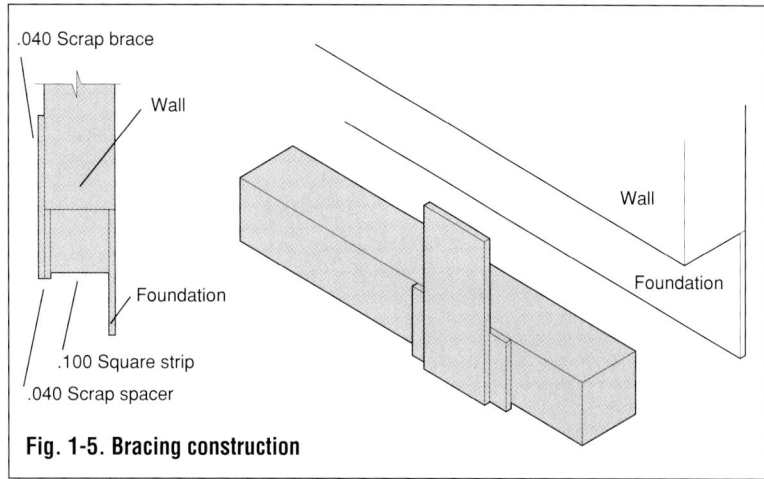

Fig. 1-5. Bracing construction

from sheet styrene. These were 7/8" high and the full length of the 12" .040 sheet. I began adding at the rear wall since I could use a full length there; I then cut the rest to size as I went around the lower edge of the walls. I added 3/16" square braces in the three corner joints and .100 square braces to join the foundation to the bottoms of the walls. I placed the foundation flush with the outer surface of the brick walls with the .100 squares at the joint. Remember, the walls are about 3/16" thick and my foundation is only .040 thick. I also added small scraps of .040 on top of the .100 square braces. I added larger strips to this and to the inner walls; I did this in at least three places on each of the

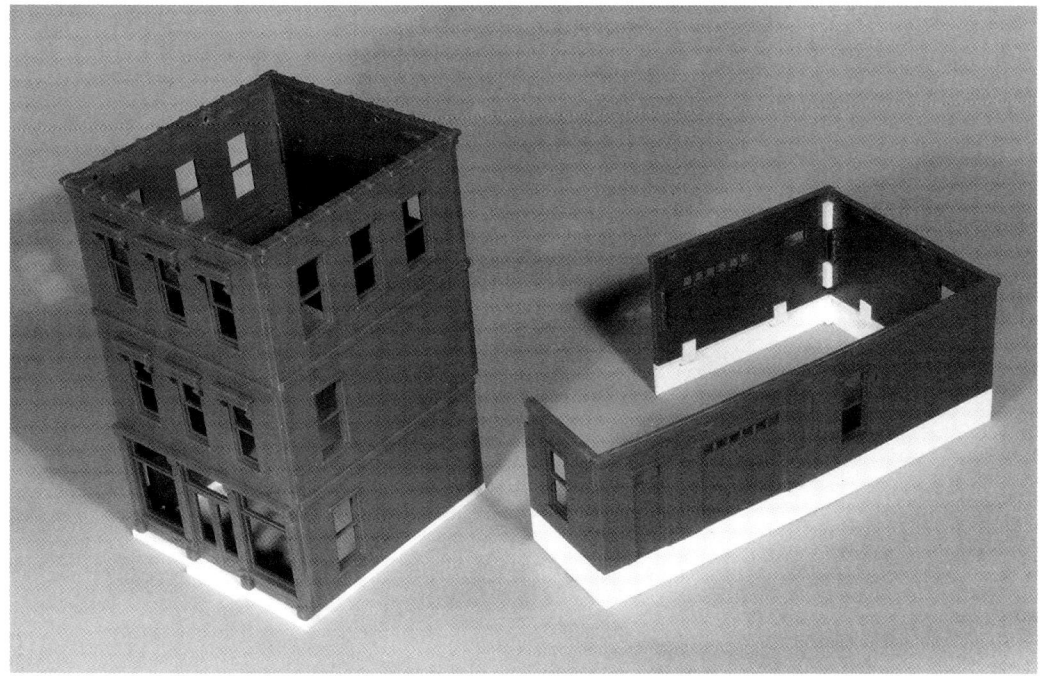

Fig. 1-6. This shows the foundation added below both units.

larger walls and in two places on the short one. This extra bracing really secures the foundation to the walls firmly (see fig. 1-5).

I also added a low foundation beneath the main building walls. Here I used 3/16" square strips that were flush with the inside of the walls. On the front I used a second strip bonded to the first. This is necessary because that wall is thicker because of the fancy front extending out a little farther than the other walls on the first floor. I added a shorter third strip just in front of the entrance to make a step. (Both foundations are shown in fig. 1-6.)

ATTACHING THE ADDITION

In order to bond the two units together, I had to cut a notch in the vertical brick on the side wall so I could place the addition wall, which was now taller, flush against it. Here I used a knife with a large chisel blade. I also had to cut a small section from the top of the short addition wall so it would fit flush against the rear wall. My notch was a little over 5/8" from the top and the thickness of the wall, which is about 3/16". I cut it a little smaller and filed the notch as needed until I got a snug fit.

I used scraps of unused foundation strips to bond the small addition wall to the main side wall on the inside and similar strips at the walls where the addition joins the other main side wall. I also bonded the foundation to these walls with short strips of .125 x .188 strip stock. Also, I added additional braces wherever I felt they would help hold everything together (see fig. 1-7).

THE STAIRS

Since the doors were now raised I needed to provide some steps to reach them. I made two sets of steps from 3/16" square strip stock. I used my NorthWest Short Line Chopper tool to cut 3/4" segments. The Chopper will not cut through the 3/16" strip, so I scored each side of the strip and snapped the segments off at the score marks (see fig. 1-8). If you do not have a Chopper, just score each segment with a knife, keeping the scores as square as possible. My steps were four high, so I needed ten segments for each set of steps (see fig. 1-9). I bonded four segments together, stacked three on top of the last segment, and then the rest in stair fashion. I let these set up a while, and when they had set solid, I filed the sides smooth. I bonded one set to the front below the small door.

THE LOADING DOCK

I made a loading dock at the rear to serve the rail siding. It is made from leftover .040 foundation strips and has a top made from .060 sheet. My dock top measures 1 1/4" deep by 5 1/4" wide. I assembled the foundation strips around the .060 top.

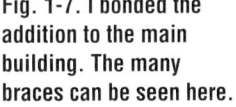

Fig. 1-7. I bonded the addition to the main building. The many braces can be seen here.

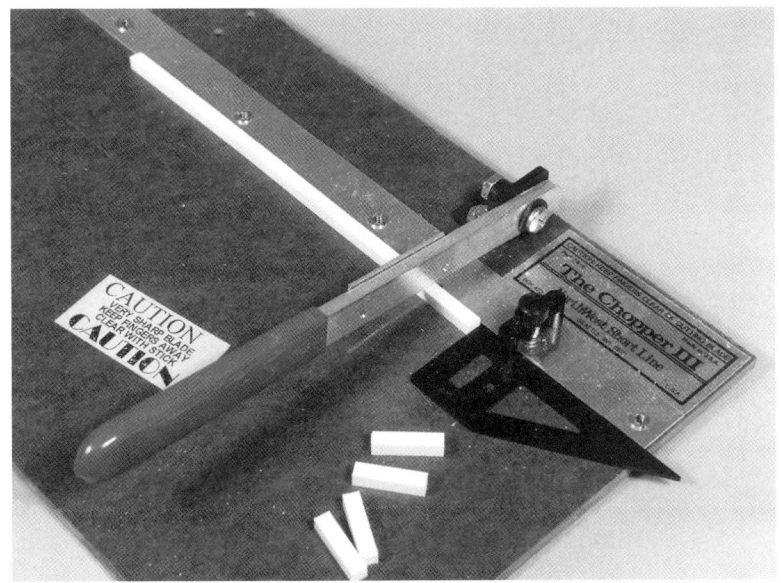

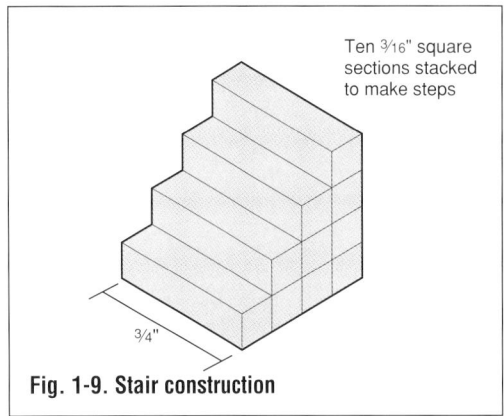

Fig. 1-9. Stair construction

Fig. 1-8. I used the Chopper to cut the ¾"-long stair treads used to make the steps.

I then braced it in the corners and at the joint of the top and sides with ³⁄₁₆" and .100 square strip, respectively. I added a brace underneath the center of the dock for extra support.

THE INEVITABLE SNAG

It seems that there is always one problem that sneaks in on a project. Mine involved my rear addition wall, which bowed out in the middle. Here's a way to fix it and at the same time hide the butt joint between the two segments of the rear wall of the addition.

To pull the center of the rear wall in toward the main building, I added a piece of .047-diameter music wire as a brace. I first drilled two holes, one right through the joint about ½" down from the top and one about ½" up from the bottom in the foundation. Then I bent the music wire ends 90 degrees so the wire would go in these two holes. The top part of the wire was long enough so it would reach over to the side wall of the main building. The bottom part of the wire went in about ⅜" through the foundation hole. Next, I drilled a hole in the side wall, bent the wire 90 degrees and inserted the end into this hole, thus pulling the rear wall toward the main building and removing the bow. I had to make sure the hole in the side wall was at the right place to allow the wire to pull in the rear wall just the right amount to straighten it. The wire is below the level of the roof, which is why I drilled the first hole ½" down from the top of the wall (see fig. 1-10). The wire looked like a pipe or conduit and hid the butt joint behind it. This is another example of how to turn a negative into a plus.

With this problem fixed, I could now add the loading dock. I had to file a notch in the rear of the dock top so the wire could go in the notch and allow me to place the dock flush against the foundation. I bonded the dock in place using braces at the joints with the foundation wall. Then I bonded the second set of steps in the corner near the small door.

THE ROOF

I used the kit roof on the main building but had to make a roof for the addition

Fig. 1-10. This wire brace pulled the bow in the rear wall toward the main building.

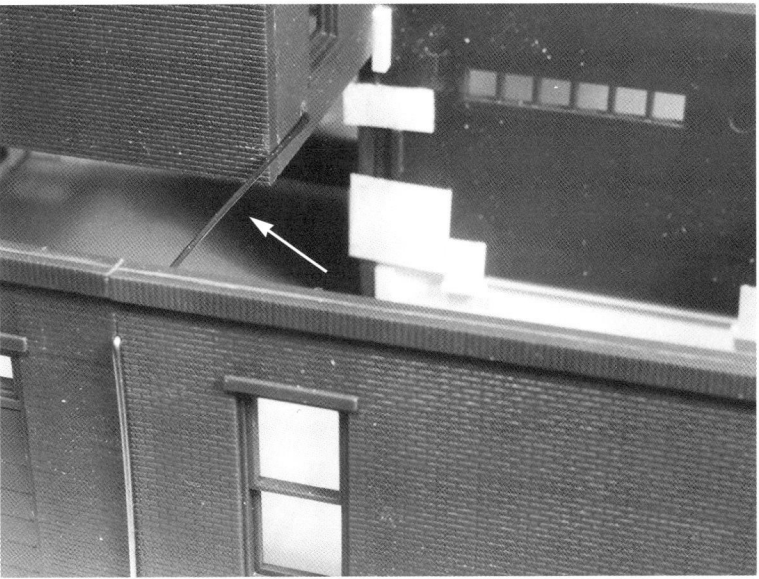

17

Fig. 1-11. This view shows the roof and loading dock added to the addition.

Fig. 1-12. Here you can see the square tubing and felt-tipped pen used to make window and roof vents.

My roof had a few gaps where it met the insides of the walls. Some of this was because the backs of the walls were a little wavy. To hide these gaps I added thin strips of styrene around the edge at the joint. I used .020 x .060 strips here, but the exact size isn't crucial as long as the gap is closed somewhat. These smaller strips flex and follow the waves better to close these gaps.

DETAILS AND A DASH OF PAINT

Now I began thinking of ways to make this look as much like a factory as I could. First I added a few vents and pipes made from Evergreen tubing. I bought a packet of assorted tubing, which included different sizes plus some styrene rod. I added a tall stack made from a 10" length of 7/16"-diameter Evergreen tubing with a 1/2" high band of 1/2"-diameter tubing bonded around the bottom. I placed this band 1/2" up from the bottom of the 7/16" tubing. This extra 1/2" base provided me with more gluing surface than the thin wall of the 7/16" tubing provided. I had to buy these pieces separately. I placed this stack on the addition roof by drilling a hole and enlarging it with a reamer then placed the 7/16" part that protruded below the band into the hole in the roof.

I assembled a Korber Models no. 930 rooftop water tank and added it to the main roof. I substituted some Plastruct tubing I had on hand for the kit's wooden pipe in the center of the tank.

The dandy ductwork on the top of the addition roof is 1/4" square strip stock. The ducts lead to a blower made from the tip of a felt-tipped marker. I added a stack on

from .060 sheet. I made a template from a piece of thin cardboard that I could easily cut and fit with scissors. Then I transferred this to my .060 sheet and cut it to that size, dropped it in place, and bonded it to the inside of the walls with some .100 square braces at the joints. Figure 1-11 shows the roofs in place along with some of the roof details.

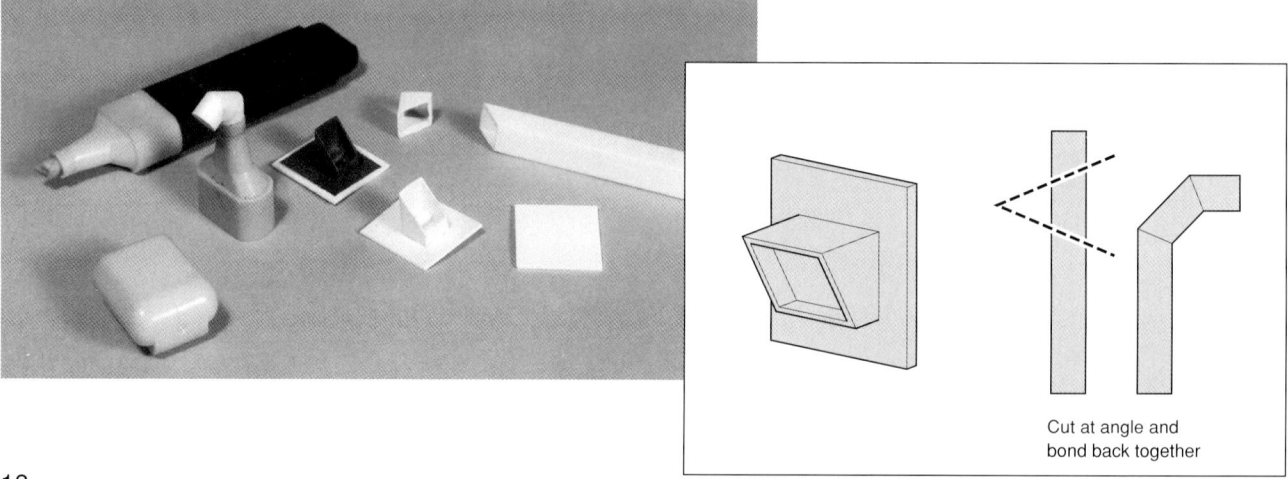

Cut at angle and bond back together

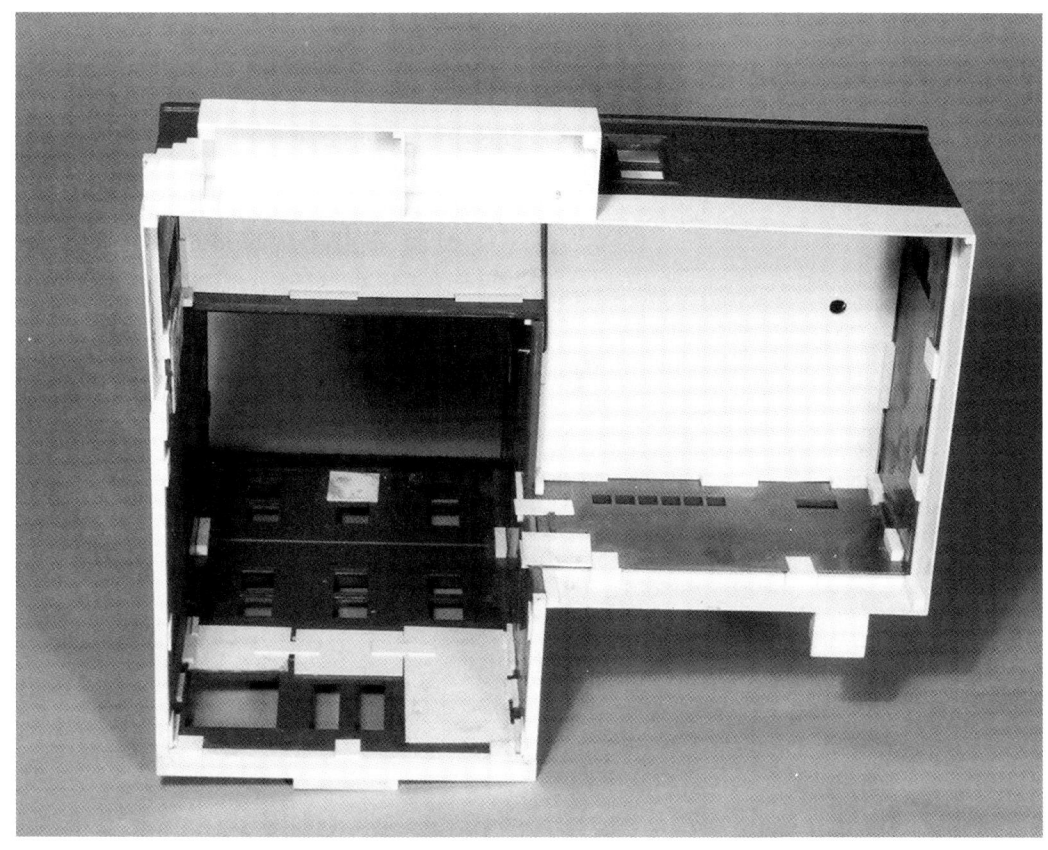

Fig. 1-13. In this view of the underside of the building, you can clearly see the interior bracing, loading dock, and blocked-up front windows and foundations.

top of this by cutting the ¼" tubing at an angle and then bonding the pieces back together again. I added a similar vent on the main roof.

I used ⅜" Plastruct square tubing to make an angled duct running from the second floor side to the addition roof. I cut the tubing at 45-degree angles at each end. I used up the ends by bonding them to a rectangle of .040 sheet and placed these in the upper parts of three windows. I liked these simple window vents so much I actually made three of them. (See fig. 1-12 for some of the ingredients.)

I thought the huge storefront windows were too open and revealed too much of the inside of the building. That meant I would have to do a lot of interior detailing. Instead, I cut some rectangles of .040 sheet and added them behind the three spaces above the large windows and doorway. I cut one to fit the large left window and the smaller one above it (see fig. 1-13). I found a spray can of red primer that matched the wall color exactly and painted these coverings and the three window vents prior to bonding them in place from inside. I made certain there would be a small portion of the horizontal window sash uncovered so I could bond window glass to it later.

I painted the roofs, including the insides of the walls that rise above the roof, and the tops of the addition walls Floquil grimy black. I painted the brick portion of the walls with a wash of Floquil Southern Pacific Daylight red with a little antique white added to make it appear faded. I used silver paint on some of the pipes, vents, and stack and used black on others.

Next, I added a wash of Floquil Polly-S white to the brick portion of the walls. I

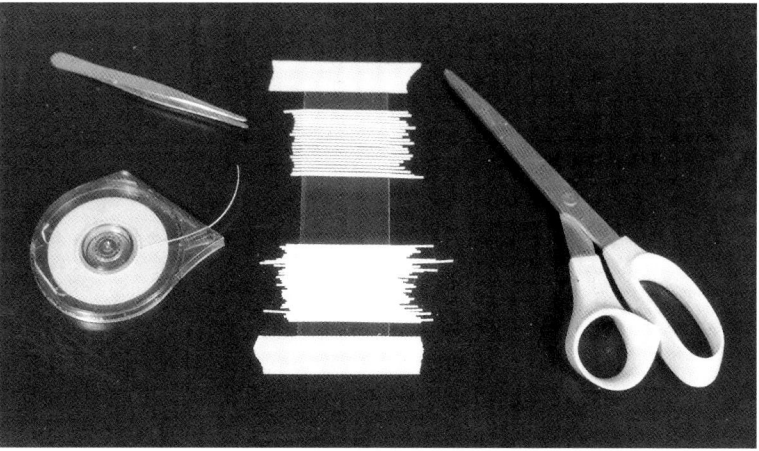

Fig. 1-14. You need tape, clear styrene, scissors, and tweezers to make the Venetian blinds.

Fig. 1-15. There is plenty of activity at the loading dock after a boxcar full of materials has departed.

painted the concrete foundations and loading dock with Floquil antique white. I gave the building a spray of Testor's Dullcote and then added a wash of alcohol and black ink to the concrete parts. Then I added clear windows cut from .015 clear Evergreen sheet styrene and bonded a few paper shades behind most of the windows.

Even after blocking off most of the front windows, I was still faced with one very large front window. To hide the barren interior, I made a Venetian blind by taking 1/16"-wide white self-adhesive tape (which I purchased in an art supply store) and placed strips side by side over a piece of .015 clear styrene. I did this so the spacing would be even and straight. I made the styrene larger than the window so I could trim it to width and have some extra above and below to fasten it in place. Then I removed every other strip with small tweezers and added two pieces of white thread vertically to represent the rope from which the blinds hang. I bonded the thread ends to the clear styrene that extended beyond the top and bottom of the blinds. I cut the blinds to fit the window width and bonded them behind the window to the back of the .040 filler that covered the small window (see fig. 1-14).

SIGNAGE

Last I added the three signs denoting the occupants of this building. I made them on my computer and printed them on blue paper. I cut the signs into rectangles and bonded them to .040 sheet styrene by flowing Testor's liquid cement through the paper. Then I cut out the styrene, leaving a small border surrounding the blue paper. You can glue the signs permanently in place on the walls.

CONCLUSION

It's amazing how a mere doodle can turn out such a different building in such a short time—one that originally had a 6" x 6" footprint but now is 9" x 12", more than double the original size. It has a more interesting look, too, since it is not just a plain box shape anymore.

A typical small brick combination freight and passenger depot

2 A Small Brick Depot

This brick depot is the second doodle brought to life, the focal point of a typical small town. It is relatively easy to make if you refer to the "Practical Doodling" sidebar in the Introduction and fig. 2-1.

I took full advantage of the modular walls offered by Design Preservation Models (DPM) to make this depot. The walls come in packets of two, so I bought one packet each of the following: no. 901-03, a blank wall; no. 901-04, a wall with a center door and a window on each side of it; no. 901-05, a wall with three windows; no. 901-06, a wall with two double windows; and no. 901-07, a wall with a large freight door. There are two other walls available if you want a fancier depot. They are exactly like the no. 901-04 and no. 901-05 walls, except that they

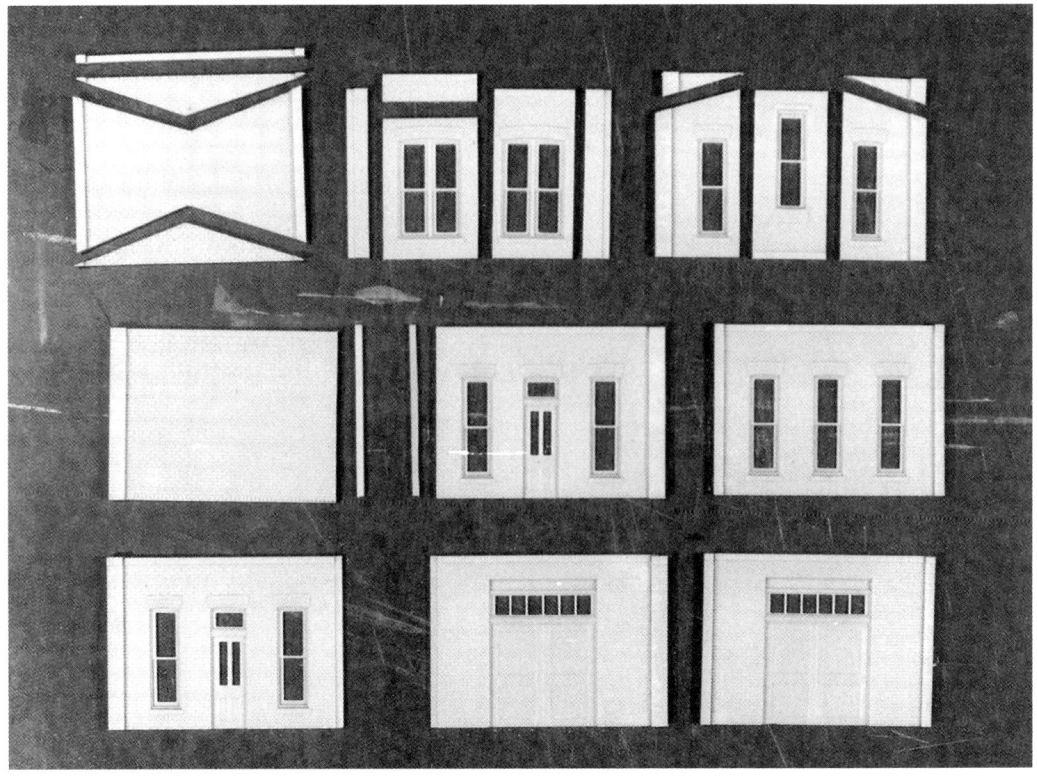

Fig. 2-1. Here you can see the walls of the depot and the pieces that have been cut from the main modular walls. You can also see each piece's relationship to the wall from which it was cut.

Fig. 2-2. I cut the walls with a knife guided by a steel ruler. Make several passes with the knife to deepen the groove.

Fig. 2-3. Next, I used the razor saw to complete the cut, guided by the knife groove.

have fancier, rounded arches over the windows and door. I used plainer arches so they would all be consistent.

CUTTING AND ARRANGING THE WALLS

Figure 2-1 shows the walls laid out with the pieces I cut from them pulled slightly apart. You can see where each piece comes from in relation to the original wall. When I reassemble the new parts, they should all fit just as if they were kit parts.

Prior to cutting any walls, I bonded the pilasters in place and let them set up for a while, so they actually became a part of the wall to which they were fastened. Figures 2-2, 2-3, and 2-4 show how I cut the walls.

Before adding the pilasters, I made certain that the wide ones were on all the walls that would become the front and back walls and the narrow pilasters were on the two walls that would become the end walls. I followed the clear instructions provided in each packet.

The only difficult part of making a DPM building is filing the many corner edges to a 45-degree angle. To accomplish this, hold the wall between two fingers and the thumb of one hand and scrape away the plastic using a knife with a no. 11 blade.

Fig. 2-4. Once the pieces are cut and angled the walls look almost like a kit.

Fig. 2-5. The front and rear walls in position for bonding. The pen points to the place where one wall had to be adjusted to make the rear wall the same length as the front wall. Note that the rear wall is slightly longer than the front wall; some material must be removed from the back wall pieces to make both the same length.

Hold the blade 90 degrees to the wall and scrape back and forth from finger to thumb. This will remove plastic much more quickly than filing and almost naturally makes a 45-degree bevel. All you need to file are the edges next to the finger and thumb where the knife does not reach the edges. (Make certain that the blade is secured tightly in the knife. I tighten the blade each time I use it. This may sound dangerous, but I still have ten fingers after doing it for many, many years.) See fig. 2-4.

Figure 2-5 shows the rear and front walls placed next to each other. Note that the rear wall is a little longer than the front. I needed to determine the actual width of the bay before cutting this wall piece to final size. I cut out a small section at the spot indicated by the pen point.

THE AGENT'S BAY WINDOW

The agent's bay window is the one thing that adds distinction to this depot but is the most difficult part to make. You may choose to skip this feature and substitute a no. 901-04 wall for the front; in the rear, you may choose either a second no. 901-05 wall or a second no. 901-04.

If you decide to go ahead with the bay, as I did, use the wide pilasters on the small side-window walls and none on the double-window wall in the front.

Figure 2-6 is a full-sized template of the formers around which I assembled my angled bay. These two formers are made

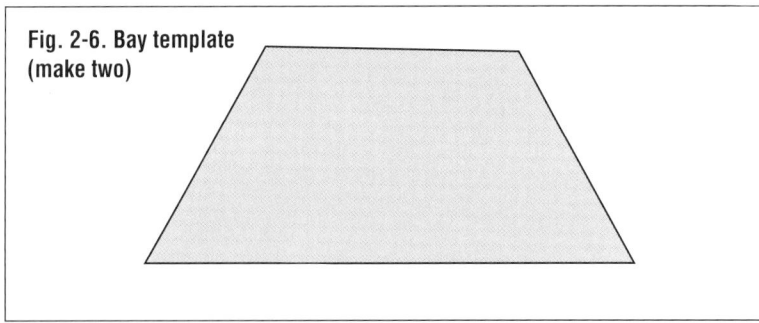

Fig. 2-6. Bay template (make two)

Fig. 2-7. This photo shows the bay unit assembled around the two formers.

Fig. 2-8. I filed the back of the bay unit on sandpaper to get it flat.

from .060 sheet styrene. I used one as a subfloor and the other one to make a false ceiling. The subfloor and ceiling formers helped hold the bay together as a unit once I bonded the walls of the bay around them. I used .080 square strip as braces in the joints between the formers and the walls.

After bonding the bay to the two formers, and after the assembly had set up for more than an hour, I filed the back of the side walls at an angle. They were then flat against the glue tabs of the main walls to which they would be fastened, as shown in fig. 2-7. I did this by rubbing the bay unit over a sheet of coarse sandpaper (see fig. 2-8).

AN OPTIONAL BAY

To add another kind of bay, place the side walls of the bay at right angles to the main walls. However, this might make the bay stick out too far. You can use the narrower part of the no. 901-06 two-windowed wall as the front of the bay and the wider part to fill the gap in the rear wall. You can also narrow the two bay side walls by sawing a section of brick about 3/8" wide off the pilaster end and then bonding the walls back together again. This would narrow the bay side walls.

OTHER OPTIONS

You now have three options for the front of the depot: an angled bay, as I did, a bay at right angles, or no bay at all. There are other options that I did not include in my doodles. For instance, you can swap the freight door on the end with the blank wall, thus placing the large door at the rear of the depot. Or you can purchase a second packet of three-window walls (no. 901-05) and replace the blank wall with a windowed wall. You might even consider making an all-passenger depot by using only windowed walls and making a separate freight house. DPM's many wall options allow for this flexibility.

WALL ASSEMBLY

The "kit" parts I made were now ready for assembly. I assembled my station by bonding the bay unit to the front walls, keeping everything as square as possible.

Fasten the cut-off ends of the bay side walls to the glue tab on the adjacent main walls. There is a row of vertical bricks on top of all of the walls. In order to allow the bay side walls to fit against the glue tabs, you must file the edge of the vertical brick off the bay side walls. You need file only a little bit for a good fit at these inside corner joints.

I bonded the bay to the gluing tabs of the adjacent main walls. I added full-length braces along the front wall at the top and bottom using 1/8" square strip stock. Next, I assembled the rear wall by combining the four pieces used here. I fit the double window and the single window

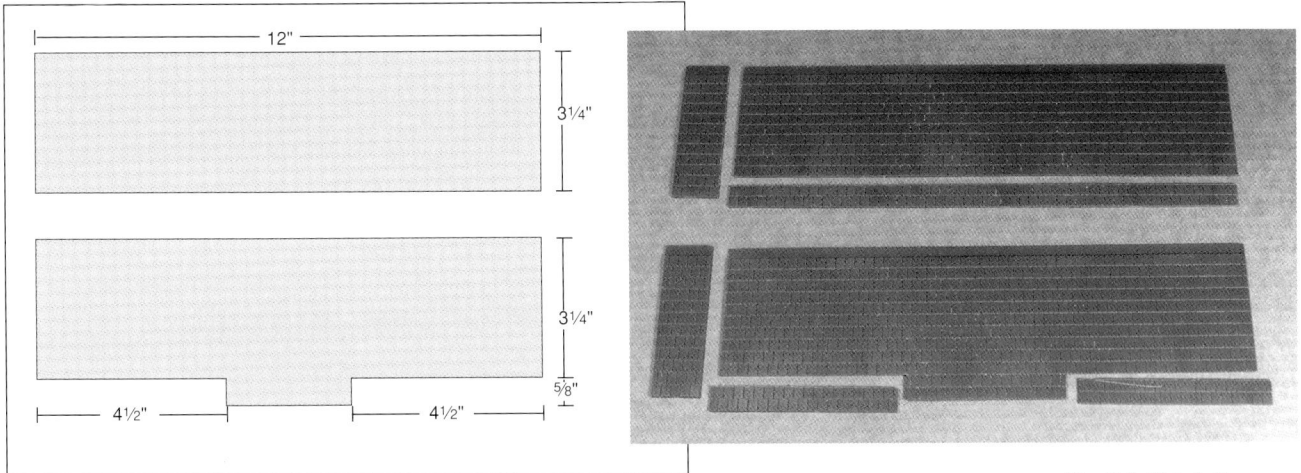

Fig. 2-9. This is the Bigg roof, with the ends and part of the rear and front trimmed to fit the new building.

side by side to fill the gap between the full width pieces at each end. Here is where you may need to do a little filing or adjusting of the width to get these pieces to fit. I made the adjustment to that one section by removing about 3/8" from one end of the two-window wall so the rear wall length matched the front (see fig. 2-5).

These joints do not have any pilasters to disguise them. If they are too noticeable, you can hide them by adding a piece of wire to represent conduit at these areas after all the joints have set up solidly. I did this on one joint by making a long, U-shaped wire with the ends inserted in holes drilled in the joint, one near the top and one near the bottom.

I also used full-length braces at the top and bottom on this wall. I then added the peaks to the two end walls and bonded my four walls together. I used 3/16" and 1/8" square strip braces in each of the corner joints, which helps keep things square and adds strength.

If you chose one of the other options, you will need different window combinations to fill the gap in the rear wall. (You will have an unused no. 901-06 wall to cut apart, if you need it.)

AN ECONOMY ROOF

There are three ways to make a roof for this depot. One is to use up any leftovers from another kit. That's what I did, so I didn't have to buy anything extra. I had roof pieces left over from making Bigg Industries (see Chapter 6). There were plenty of pieces to cover the depot. When I had decided to replace Bigg's roof, I thought it did not look much like a shingle roof because the shingles were too big. It begin looking more and more like a slate roof. I was fooled by the greenish color, and if painted the right color, it could represent slate. Figure 2-9 shows where this roof had to be cut down in order to fit my depot. You will have pieces of different lengths, depending on whether you have chosen one of the other options (different bays change the length). Don't attach the roof to the walls until later, when the painting is done.

I removed the raised guides for placing the original kit rafters to the underside of the roof. I used a chisel blade and then filed the area smooth (see fig. 2-10). Then I cut five formers or "rafters" from .040 sheet, using the end peaks as a template to get the right pitch. (These are also shown in fig. 2-11.) I bonded the roof halves to the formers, making sure the formers were inside the end walls and their ends cleared the side walls. This makes a removable roof (see fig. 2-12). It could be bonded to the walls if you wish,

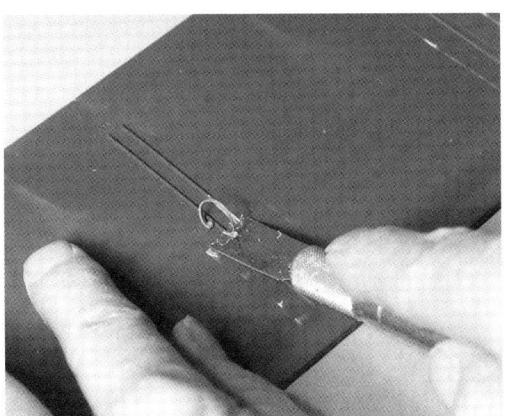

Fig. 2-10. I used a large chisel blade to remove the cast-on roof eave guides.

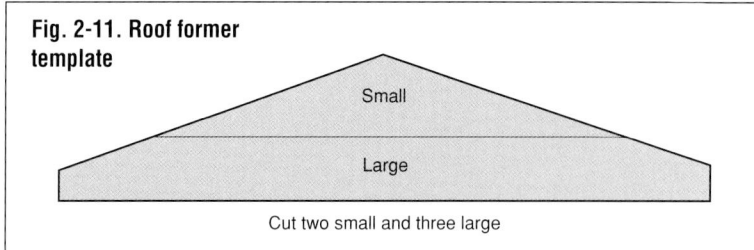

Fig. 2-11. Roof former template

Small
Large
Cut two small and three large

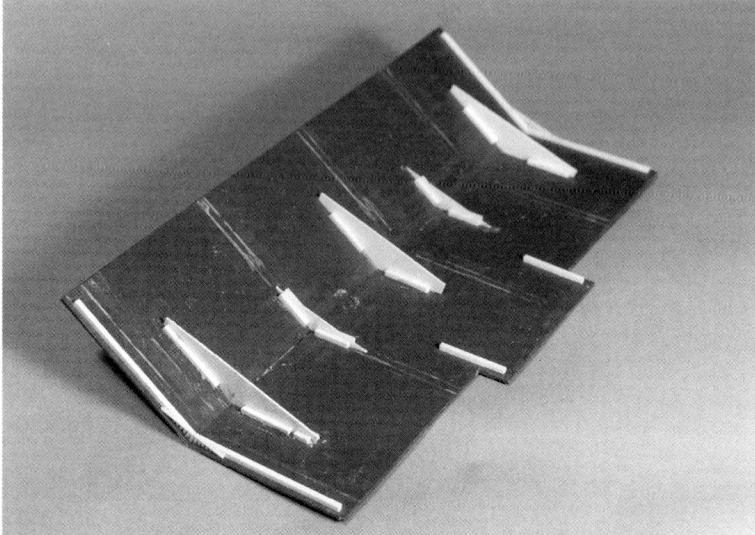

Fig. 2-12. The five roof braces in place on the underside of the roof.

Fig. 2-13. The Atlas HO scale picket fence is cut by striking a single-edge razor blade with a small hammer.

strips of bond paper or a full-sized piece of facial tissue (one layer) about 5/8" wide and add them to represent asphalt roll roofing. Begin at the bottom and overlap each successive strip as you progress to the top, stopping at the two .020 x 188 strips. Cut the top of the final roofing strip so it butts against these strips. If you use bond paper strips, paint Testor's cement on top; it will go right through and bond the strips to the roof. Paint it later. If you use the tissue, paint Floquil grimy black on top. This will also act as a glue by going right through the tissue to the roof.

For the third option, bond Plastruct asphalt shingle material to the .060 sheet subroof.

SOME DETAILS

The first detail I added to the depot was a Grandt Line chimney with a new cap made from a square of .080 styrene with a small length of tubing on top. I cut an opening in the roof peak so I could insert the chimney. To add it somewhere else, cut the bottom of the chimney to match the roof pitch and bond it in place. I made a soil pipe from two pieces of small-diameter tubing, drilled a hole in the roof, and inserted the chimney in the hole. The roof gets some eave trim at the ends. Here I used .100 x .100 strip bonded to the underside of the roof and set back a little from the actual roof edge. I added two similar short strips at the edges of the roof overhanging the agent's bay (see fig. 2-12).

The fancy triangular detail at the end of each peak is a section of Atlas HO scale picket fence as seen in fig. 2-13. Although I did not add them, you can add roof braces at the four corners and a few across the front and back walls.

THE COAL BOX

I made the coal box from Evergreen .040 thick V-groove siding with .100 spacing. It is roughly 7/8" wide by 5/8" deep with sloped side walls. I counted boards and got them as close to the 5/8" x 7/8" measurement as I could without cutting any boards in half. (See fig. 2-14 for the general assembly procedure.) The side walls are bonded inside the front and rear walls. The lid is the same material. The small top is a board and a half and is placed flush with the back of the rear wall of the box. I made a false bottom from scraps

but not yet. I added a new copper roof cap, since the cap from the Bigg roof was at a sharper pitch. Here I used .030 x .250 styrene strips, one on each roof half. I added a piece of 1/16" Evergreen rod down the center.

A NEW ROOF

For the second roof option, cut two pieces of plain .060 sheet styrene to the dimensions shown in fig. 2-9 and add this to the peaks. File the top edges a bit to get a better fit, and then add strips of .020 x .188 Evergreen at the top. Then cut

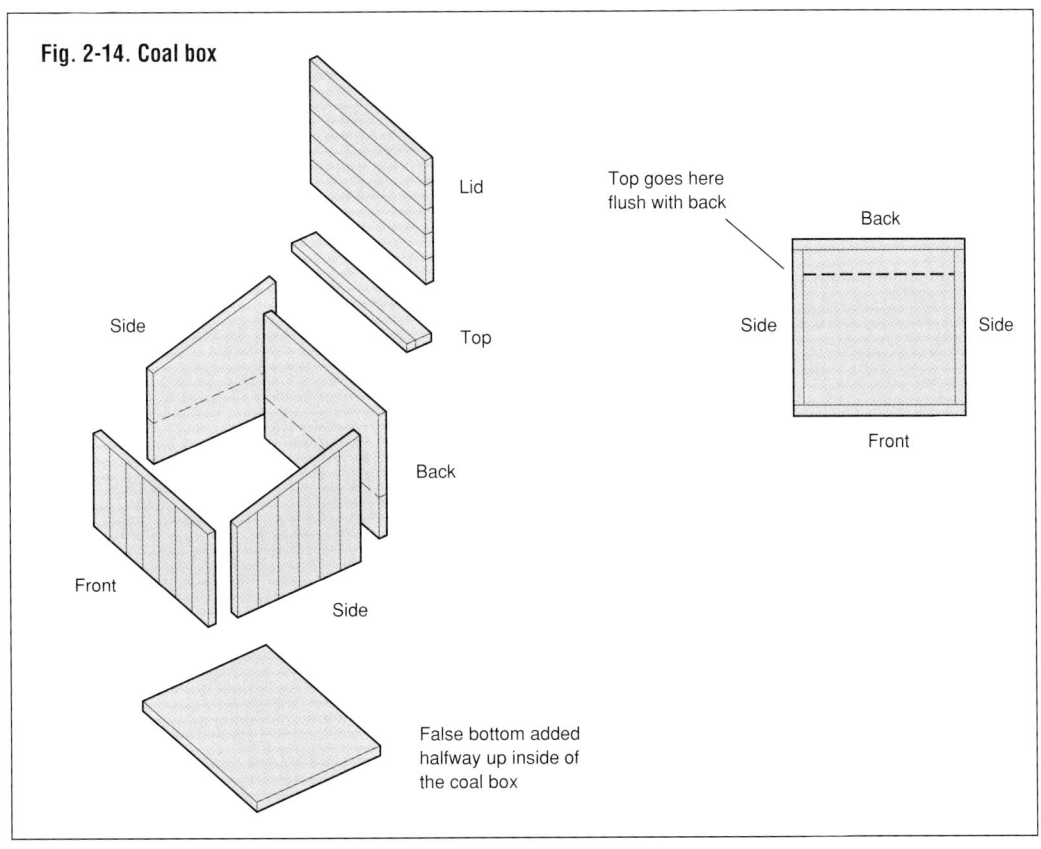

Fig. 2-14. Coal box

and placed it about halfway up the inside of the box walls. Then I added some coal to this by bonding it on with thinned white glue.

You could make the coal box simpler by having the lid closed, or add a pair of hinges to the top of the lid. I liked the look of the open box.

A RESTING PLACE

This little depot needed a platform, so I made one from .040 sheet styrene cut an

Fig. 2-15. The bay, the interior bracing, the window glass, the shades, the wire conduit, and the coal box are all clearly visible in this photo.

Fig. 2-16. The rear of the depot is plainer, but just what you see as you head for the train that is about to arrive. There is just enough interesting detail surrounding a small depot to create a lot of memories. It looks like the agent had to hurry back to his desk, since he has left the lid of the coal box up.

inch larger than the depot all the way around. I added ¼" square strips all around the bottom edges and a few across the center. File the edges smooth after the strips have been bonded on and set up. This represents a concrete platform. I scribed in some large squares with my knife and then added a few cracks and some chips or nicks to show some wear. I bonded the depot to the platform after completing the painting.

I placed my depot off-center toward the rear and the left. This left more room in front of the two large freight doors for maneuvering baggage wagons and general loading.

PAINTING

I've saved painting for last, although you can paint some parts as you go. I waited until the building was assembled and painted the doors and windows Floquil roof brown. Combined with the buff-colored brick walls, this was in keeping with the look established by the Rico depots (see Chapter 4). I also painted the eaves, end trim, and coal box with the same brown.

One trick that can only be done with styrene buildings is to scrape off any paint that ends up some place you don't want it to be. I scraped off some of the brown that went astray while painting some of the windows. Using a sharp chisel or new pointed blade, just scrape the paint until the bare plastic shows through again.

I mixed a little Floquil Great Northern blue and some white with a little grimy black and painted the top or slate portion of the roof. I painted the roof cap with Floquil patina since this was supposed to be an oxidized copper cap. If you can't find patina, Penn Central or Great Northern green will do. I painted the platform Floquil antique white to represent concrete. Next, I brushed the brick walls, the roof, and the platform with an alcohol and black ink wash, which settled into the mortar grooves and cracks in the platform and brought out the individual bricks and cracks. Then I sprayed on Testor's Dullcote. Last, I added the window glass using clear styrene and some buff-colored paper shades in the windows. Figure 2-15 shows some of the interior bracing, the window glass, the shades, the wire conduit, and the coal box at the rear.

CONCLUSION

This kitmingle filled my need for a small brick depot. It also represents another way to demonstrate how the doodling ideas can work magic when used to design a kitmingled building.

A typical block of stores with signs. Some fronts are detailed with interiors and others have curtains to hide the bare interiors.

3 A Block of Stores

It seems many small towns have a Railroad Avenue or Depot Street opposite the railroad station. There usually are a few stores located on that street, since at one time it was the commercial focal point of the town. In some cases the town grew from this small beginning and in other cases this street is the whole town. On a small model railroad the latter is generally the case because a town takes up a lot of space.

As one of my doodles shows, I set out to make a typical block of stores to occupy Railroad Avenue. I used two Walthers Nicole's Java Huts and a Toy Shoppe as the basis of my block. In the real world, sometimes a block will have different buildings, and at other times they will be built with a similar look. There is a little bit of each in this block.

THE BASIC IDEA

The kits I used are ideal for kitmingling this block since they provide extra parts. I used those parts to stretch three kits into seven small stores. Each kit uses common bases, side and rear walls, chimneys, and roofs. The fronts are the only parts that are different.

I assembled one of each kit, which is easy because they are cleverly designed to snap together precisely (see fig. 3-1). This

29

Fig. 3-1. This photo of the two assembled kits shows the two buildings that will form the basis of the block.

Fig. 3-2. In this Java Hut, I cut wall A into three main segments. I also cut the two door openings out of the corners of the plain segment.

showed me exactly what I had to work with. I then disassembled the kits so I could cut them apart later.

EXTRA! EXTRA! EXTRA!

In each kit there is a sprue containing the windows and doors and one storefront. A second sprue contains another storefront and a bay window. The third sprue contains a set of signs and a cornice. These three sprues are molded in tan in the Java Hut kit and in white in the Toy Shoppe kit (except for the tan sign sprue).

The window sprue contains windows and doors for both kits, so some will be left over. To a kitmingler, having all these extra parts is like discovering a gold mine—all those free parts are just begging to be used!

Add to this bonanza the thought that any wall that will not be seen can be used elsewhere. That's how I found new fronts to place on top of the extra storefronts and new rear walls for the expanded buildings. (Refer to the "Practical Doodling" sidebar in the Introduction to see where walls that will not be seen could be cut up to provide extra wall material.) Remember that these buildings will be placed side by side with no space in between, so there are plenty of large places on walls A, B, C, and D to get what I need.

WHERE TO BEGIN

I began by cutting side wall A of the Java Hut horizontally, at a point three rows of bricks above the curved brick arch of the windows. Note that I did not cut all the way to the rear end but stopped 1/4" in from the rear. Next, I cut vertically from 1/4" in from the edge down to the bottom. You must keep this 1/4"-wide strip of the wall intact because the rear wall in these kits goes between the side walls and the side walls go behind and against the front wall.

This 1/4"-wide strip is needed to keep the Java Hut square when assembling it. Figure 3-2 shows the first Java Hut and the wall pieces I removed from the A wall side.

I cut wall B on the second Java Hut kit exactly the same way, but without cutting the two door openings. Now I could assemble both Java Huts using the snap tabs, although I actually bonded everything with liquid cement except the storefront in the second Java Hut. There, I cut off the door and bonded it in place permanently. (I'll use the rest of the storefront later.) I was then ready to make the two new stores that fit between the two assembled Java Huts.

THE FRONT WALLS

I measured the width of the extra storefront, which came to 5", and transferred this measurement to what was originally the front side of wall A. I cut it a little wider to allow for filing the edge to a perfect fit. This was a vertical cut and I used the ends of the bricks to align my rule to ensure a perfect vertical. I cut wall B the same amount.

Next, I measured the height of the extra storefront, which was 3⅛", and cut both of the 5" wide A and B wall pieces horizontally 3⅛" from the bottom. I cut off the three tabs at the bottom of these walls since there would be no base to which to attach them.

At this point I had now sawed each of the two pieces, originally removed from walls A and B, into three segments. Both of the segments with two windows will be used above the two extra storefronts. I filed their sides so they matched the width of the storefronts.

A NEW CORNICE

It would have been great if I had some extra cornices like those above the two assembled Java Huts, but I did not, so I had to make something to fit on top of the new storefronts. Both Evergreen and Plastruct make a huge variety of strip stock in all sizes and shapes, so I gathered up a few and made a new, simpler cornice that was something like the upper trim of the extra storefronts. The diagram in fig. 3-3 shows how I arrived at my cornice. I made the cornice the full length of the strip stock, which is at least 13". The only difficult part was filing the angled edge on the long piece of .125 x .250 strip. I cut two sections of cornice 5¹⁄₁₆" long to fit over each new brick front. The extra ¹⁄₁₆"

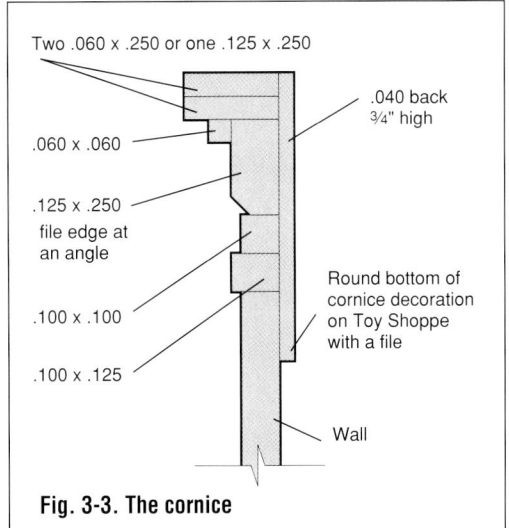

Fig. 3-3. The cornice

allowed for final trimming to make the cornices match the width of the new front. I saved the remaining section of cornice for use later.

These cornices rest on top of the new front walls, so the wall tops must be filed flat. The cornice adds about ½" to the height of the front, which is needed so the new roof will be above the cutout portions of the walls on the completed kits that are on either side of the new storefronts. This also allows the roof to have a slight slope for water runoff toward the rear of the building.

ASSEMBLY

I usually do my painting after a building is assembled, but in this case I painted some parts beforehand. I painted one storefront, two windows, and the new cornice with Floquil coach green and the brick wall with Floquil earth. I used Floquil spray paint for these tasks, but I brush-painted the second cornice, which goes above the second storefront, with a mix of Floquil paint. I used some roof brown, reefer white, and a new color called aged concrete. The largest portion was the white, and I added drops of the other colors until I matched the tan color of the kit parts.

Next I bonded the storefronts to their respective brick second floors and then added the cornices and windows. I placed the two complete storefronts side by side and bonded scrap braces behind the butt joint, being careful not to get any solvent on the painted fronts.

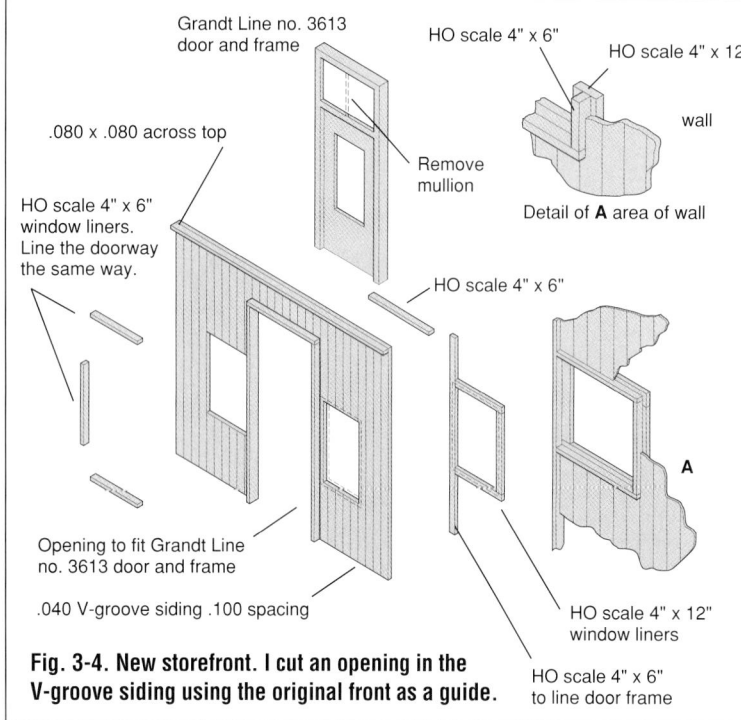

Fig. 3-4. New storefront. I cut an opening in the V-groove siding using the original front as a guide.

Fig. 3-5. The modernized front, showing the trim around the door and windows.

the building, yet gives it a look that belongs in more modern times.

For my new front I used Evergreen V-groove siding, .040 thick with .100 spacing. I used the original front as a guide for overall size and cut an opening in the V-groove siding (see fig. 3-4). I based my front around a Grandt Line no. 3613 door and its frame. I first cut an opening in the center of the V-groove siding that would accommodate the door frame plus a little more. This ensured that I could add an extra frame around the Grandt Line frame. Then I cut two window openings on each side of the door opening. I framed the openings with HO scale 4" x 6" strip stock, placing the 4" edges flush with the back of the .040 siding. Next, I added a strip of HO scale 4" x 6" stock around the door with the 4" edge flush with the inside of the door opening, and I added 4" x 12" strip around three sides of each window. This made the inside frame around the windows evenly spaced. I wound up adding a strip of 4" x 6" on top of each window and the door to hide a bad match of my 4" x 6" trim in one corner. I spray-painted this whole front silver; later I bonded the kit glass to the back of the storefront. Figure 3-5 shows the completed front.

THE REAR WALLS

Two of the remaining segments I cut from walls A and B had a window in them and were about 2 7/16" wide and 5 5/16" tall. These were the extreme ends of a new rear wall (you can see these in doodle number three). The third segments of walls A and B were each about 5" wide and 3 1/8" high and had no windows. I used these to fill the gap between the two end segments. I used one full height and placed the second on top of the first, cutting off the top so it matched the height of the two extreme end pieces. I filed all edges to get the best joints possible. There was about 1/16" extra width on the blank segments, so I had this much to play with to saw or file one or both of the ends to get a good fit, making the rear wall the same width as the front wall. I bonded scraps of styrene across all the butt joints on the inside.

I wanted some rear access doors in this wall, but I didn't have any, so I used two Grandt Line doors from kit no. 3610, which contains four Shed Doors.

1960S, HERE WE COME!

Remember that I did not add the normal storefront to the second Java Hut, but I did add the small door by cutting it from the main front. Many older stores have modernized part of their facades to be more attractive to customers. Often these fronts are aluminum or steel overlays or completely rebuilt fronts. That's what I did to this storefront—modernized it. You could do something similar to more than one store, if you wish, using the same basic techniques. Modernizing the front lets you keep the older charm of the rest of

Fig. 3-6. In this photo of the block, you can see sidewalks and interior bracing. I secured the sidewalks to the base of the walls and to the side of the base.

To make it easy to install these doors, I made a horizontal cut and a vertical cut in each corner of the blank segment in the center of the rear wall. Thus the adjoining wall became the opposite side of the door opening (see fig. 3-2).

I set this new rear wall forward about ¼" in from the rear walls of the two Java Huts on each side. Once I was satisfied with the fit of the new front and rear walls, I bonded them to their respective Java Huts. I made certain the new walls were even with the bottom of the two Java Hut bottoms.

SIDEWALKS

The Walthers kits include a sidewalk as part of the base. My new stores lacked this, so I had to make a sidewalk. I cut a strip 2½" wide by about 10 1/32" long from .040 sheet styrene. Then I added .100 square strip along both long edges and across both ends that made a sidewalk the same thickness as the originals. I scribed in individual squares with lines 1¼" apart to match the originals. Then I bonded the new sidewalk to the bottoms of the new storefronts using .100 square strips on the inside bottom of the storefront at the joint. I also added scrap braces between the kit bases and the rear of the sidewalk top that protruded behind the storefronts.

A similar sidewalk or base was needed for the back wall to rest on, so I made one in the same way but only 1¼" wide. The rear sidewalk extends out about ½" beyond the rear wall surface. Figure 3-6 shows a bird's-eye view of the assembled buildings and the many braces that hold everything together.

A NEW ROOF

The two new stores needed a roof, which I made from .040 sheet cut to fit between the taller buildings with a little overhang beyond the rear wall. Later I bonded this to the back of the front wall cornice, to the top of the rear wall, and to the walls of the Java Huts on each side. I used small segments of .100 square strip stock behind the front cornice for the roof to rest on and similar ones on the sides of the adjoining Java Huts. Once this roof is on, the four-building unit becomes fairly solid. At this point I had four stores that could stand by themselves. If this is all you have room for, skip to the section on detailing later in this chapter. Otherwise, read on for information about adding three more buildings.

THE REALLY, REALLY DIFFERENT PART OF THE BLOCK

In addition to my first four stores, I made the Toy Shoppe with two small single-story stores attached to it. I used the extra parts the Toy Shoppe provides—an extra storefront, cornice, and bay window

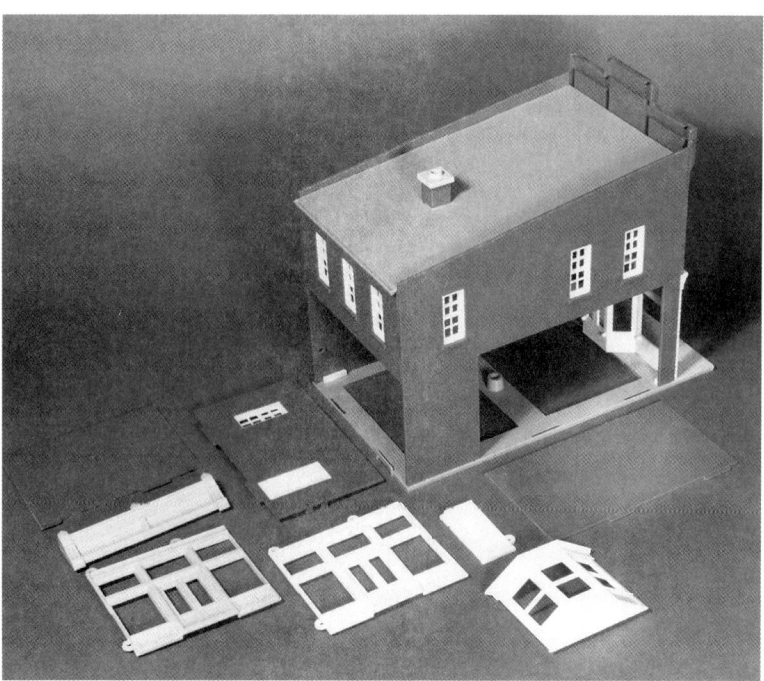

Fig. 3-7. The assembled Toy Shoppe from the rear. The walls I removed are placed next to their original location. You can clearly see the recesses in back of the upper front wall.

that were included but not needed for the Java Hut kit—to make two small single-story buildings. In order to make the sixth storefront, I made the same modifications that I made on the Java Huts. Since I used only one kit, there was not as much wall material available, so I had to compromise a bit.

First, I measured the smaller extra storefront, which was 3" high above the main area and 3⅜" wide, excluding the door on the right side, which I sawed off. (I made use of it later.) Then I cut a segment from the left side wall (wall C in my original doodle) to this size plus one inch wider, making it 5" wide. I cut this segment so there was a ½"-wide strip remaining at the front of wall C; later I would attach the front wall of the Toy Shoppe to it (see fig 3-7).

Next, I cut two 5/16"-wide vertical strips from one end of this brick wall segment. I placed these on either side of the storefront, mimicking the look of the lower part of the Java Hut front. I filed these strips flat where they were cut and bonded them to the sides of the storefront. I then used a few scrap strip braces on the inside.

I cut the extra cornice removing the narrower part to the right of the off-center vertical decoration. When you make this cut, be sure the smaller cornice matches the full width of the new front wall. If it doesn't, file off the sides of the vertical brick segments until they match. The 5/16" width is purposely a little wide to allow for this adjusting.

The cornice molding was hollow in the back, so I covered it with a piece of .040 sheet on the back. This back is ⅞" high and 4" wide, and it rises above the flat portion of the top of the cornice a little more than ⅛". I also cut off the tip of the unused decoration and centered this on the cornice top. I then bonded the cornice to the top of the storefront and spray-painted the entire front, including the bricks, with a red primer.

THE REAR WALL AND BAY WINDOW

The rest of the cutout segment was to become the rear wall of the new store, so it needed to be 4" wide to match the new front. There were no door or window openings in this segment, but I could cut these into it easily. Where do the door and window come from? Remember, I had cut off the door from the right side of the extra front. I first envisioned this door in the rear wall. Instead I made a new door. I could have purchased more Grandt Line doors or used the second set of Shed Doors in the pack I used for the other buildings. Figure 3-8 shows how I made my doors. Use this procedure to make any size or style door.

Once my door was made, I cut an opening in the rear wall for it. I did the same thing for a window using one of the more common windows as a guide for the opening's size. Prior to installation, I spray-painted the door and window the same red as the front. To keep these items stationary when hit with the spray, I taped them to a piece of cardboard with double-sided tape.

To gain this extra window, I used the extra bay window in the most obvious way, adding it to the Toy Shoppe side wall to cover up a window on the second story. Prior to final assembly of the second Java Hut, I took its front wall and placed it against the Toy Shoppe side wall where I wanted the bay window to be. Then I traced through the bay window opening, leaving a line on the wall that I could use as a guide to cut a similar opening in the side wall. I cut on this line to make the bay opening and inserted the bay window in its new home. I first cut off the four mounting lugs; note that I also cut off the sloping roof and added in its place a new flat one cut from .100 sheet. Next I removed the lower portion of the Toy Shoppe rear wall, as shown in fig. 3-7. I cut this wall to a height of 3".

ANOTHER ROOF AND SIDEWALK

This small store also needs a roof and sidewalks, which can be made the same way as before. I made the front sidewalk 2½" wide because this small store is set back ½" from the front edge of the Toy Shoppe and the other building. This building is set back because the cornice had no side where it was cut, so by recessing the store I hid this minor problem with the Toy Shoppe side wall. The small storefront and rear walls can now be bonded to the side of the Toy Shoppe wall. Then I made a roof, cut to fit from .040 sheet. I also made a small sidewalk for the back wall that acted as a base to match the height of the Toy Shoppe base. I used the same materials and methods that I used on the other sidewalks.

What about a side wall for the small store? There really is no need for one, since this building butts against the side of the Java Hut wall. However, I had lots of scrap brick wall pieces left over, so I made up a wall using all of these scraps. I did this in case I might want to place this building somewhere else. By piecing the scraps together, I made the wall look as if it once had a building against it that was torn down, leaving the motley look a wall like this would have.

THE OTHER TINY STORE

I added the seventh store to the back of the Toy Shoppe (you could add it to the far left part of the Java Hut building). When I modernized the one storefront, I had a front left over, so I used it as the front on the tiny store that faced the side street. Instead of using brick verticals on the extreme left and right, I used .125 x .250 strip stock. To get a side wall for this store, I took the lower part of the Toy Shoppe rear that I removed previously, and I pushed it back to become the side wall. This is the same thing I did in the Tipakull Manufacturing building. To make a back wall, I cut some brick material from wall D on the right side of the

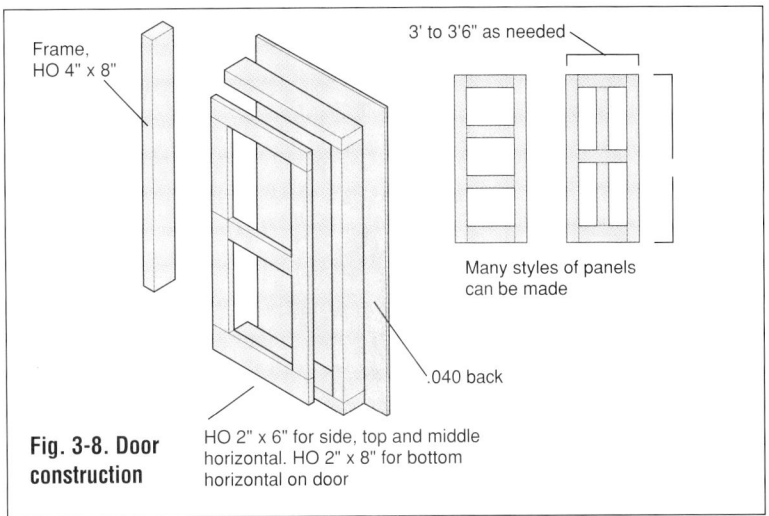

Fig. 3-8. Door construction

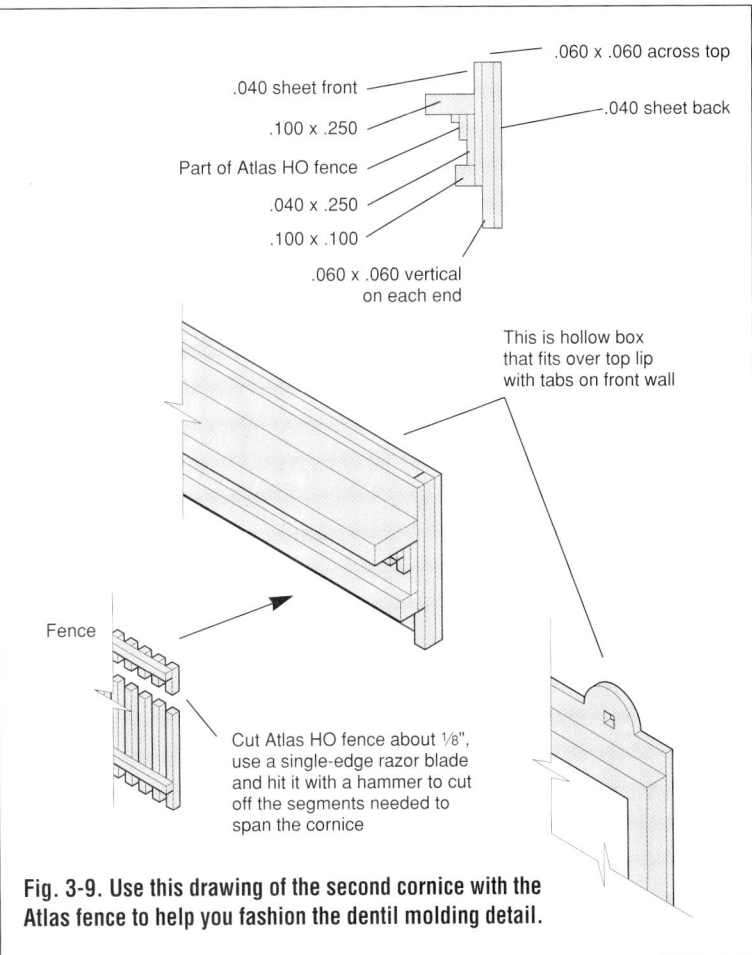

Fig. 3-9. Use this drawing of the second cornice with the Atlas fence to help you fashion the dentil molding detail.

Java Hut. This part of wall D was later covered up by the other small storefront, so the opening was not visible in the final construction.

To keep this building small, I made a new, less pretentious cornice from sheet styrene, some strip stock, and some Atlas

35

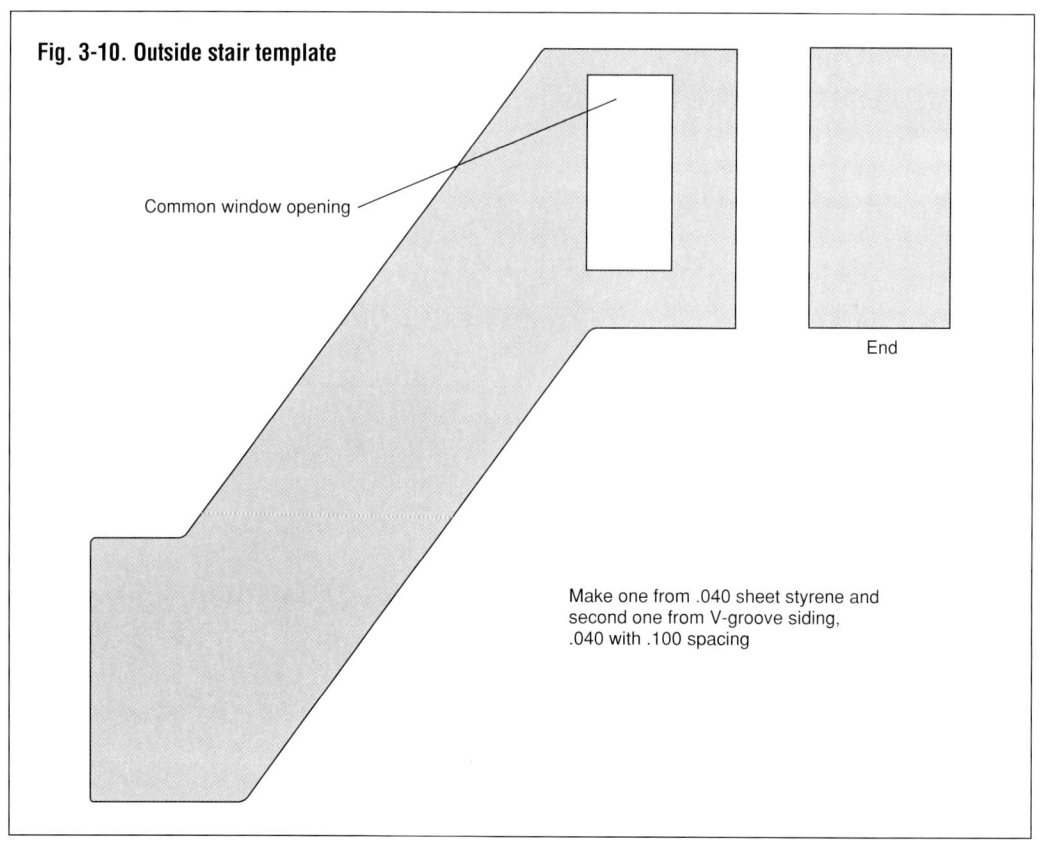

Fig. 3-10. Outside stair template

Common window opening

End

Make one from .040 sheet styrene and second one from V-groove siding, .040 with .100 spacing

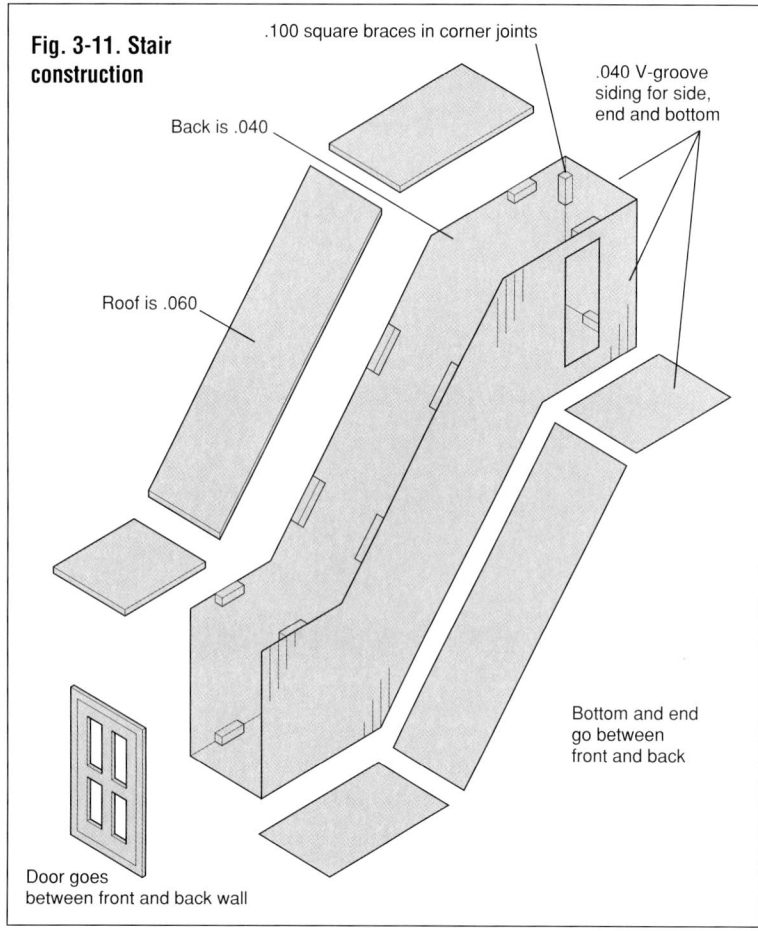

Fig. 3-11. Stair construction

.100 square braces in corner joints

.040 V-groove siding for side, end and bottom

Back is .040

Roof is .060

Bottom and end go between front and back

Door goes between front and back wall

HO scale picket fence to represent a dentil molding trim. I cut off the bottom portion of three sections of the Atlas fence between the vertical posts and joined them side by side to gain the width needed to span the cornice. Figure 3-9 shows how I assembled the cornice. I also did some painting prior to adding this store. I painted the whole front a spray green, then masked off the window and door and painted this green also. (I had already glued them into the rear wall, but it would have been easier if they had been painted before installation.) The small window was the transom that I cut from the door of the extra front. I painted this green before installation. Last, I made a roof, cut to fit, from .040 sheet styrene.

SIDEWALK TIME AGAIN!

I made another sidewalk along the side of the Toy Shoppe. I made it the same as the others, 2½" wide at the front and 3½" wide as it goes behind the rear of the store base. The length is 13¼", which meant that the last 1¼" had to be spliced, since most sheets are only 12" long. I needed this length to accommodate the store I added at the back. I made smaller bases for the side and rear of the small store just to raise them to the same height as the kit base. I filed the kit base flat on this side so the sidewalk had something to which to bond, since the bases have an angle if left alone. I also drilled holes through the .100 square strip bordering the back of the sidewalk into the kit base and inserted steel pins for extra strength.

SOME OTHER DETAILS

I added an enclosed outside stairway to the side wall of the Toy Shoppe, which not only helped secure the rather fragile sidewalk but also offered the people who have offices or live above this store access to the street without parading through the store. The Java Hut kits have this upper access door in the front but the Toy Shoppe does not. This necessity is often overlooked by most kit manufacturers.

Stairs are very difficult to construct, so I made mine the easy way: enclosed. My pseudo-stairway uses the same V-groove siding I used to modernize the one storefront and the template shown in fig. 3-10. I also made a duplicate of this shape on .040 sheet. This made it easier to construct a very odd-shaped box with a front, a back, a top (the roof), a bottom, and two ends, one of which is a door. The three-piece roof is .060 sheet with a ⅛" overhang over the V-grooved siding. Figure 3-11 also shows how everything is made. I had to make the new door at the bottom of the stairs, but that was easier than having to make the stairs themselves. The bottom of the stairs is also V-groove running vertically, even though it is not totally visible.

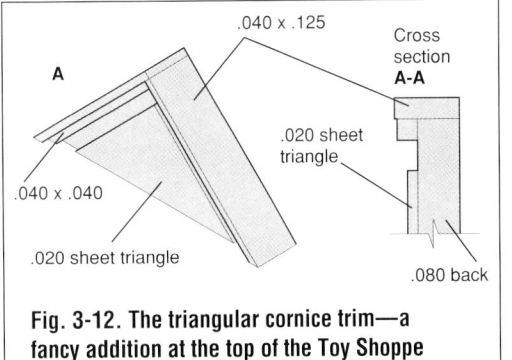

Fig. 3-12. The triangular cornice trim—a fancy addition at the top of the Toy Shoppe

Since I was blocking a window with the top of the stairs, I could make use of that window. I cut the fastening edges off of the window and filed the edges true. Then I cut a hole for the window at the top of the landing to let in some light at the head of the stairs. This window, unlike those in the brick walls, was mounted on the outside, so the opening had to be snug and the window inserted so it protruded.

The chimneys, or actually smokestacks, on the two smaller new stores were

Fig. 3-13. This rear view of the block shows the new door and window placement and how the additions relate to the main building. It also shows that the recesses in the rear of the front wall have been covered over.

Fig. 3-14. This close-up of the storefronts shows the shelves full of merchandise that invites customers to browse and shop.

I placed the saw in a groove on the flat surface and then pulled it around the edge surface. I held my saw blade so the cutting was done on what would normally be the pulling stroke with the sharp edge of the teeth pointing away from my hand. Afterwards, I cleaned up the edge with a brass-bristled brush. It took a while to do, but I felt this detail was well worth the additional time.

FANCY TOUCHES

The Toy Shoppe lacked a fancy cornice, so I thought I might try to spruce up the top a bit. I filed the tops of the four vertical pilasters flat and took some of the remaining cornice I had used on the Java Hut addition. I then cut segments of these to match the width of the four protruding vertical pilasters and filed the bottoms round. I capped the flat parts of the front wall with strip stock and made a triangular decoration from a few scraps of styrene (see fig. 3-12). If your building will be seen from the rear, you might try what I did next. There are recesses behind the raised brick areas of the front wall. I cut a piece of .020 sheet a little larger and bonded it to the back of the upper area of the front wall. It goes down to where the roof fits against the back of the front wall. After the bond set, I carved off the overhang of the .020 styrene even with the edges of the wall and finished up with a file.

To make this building less like the others, I cut the tops of the side walls parallel

lengths of Plastruct 1/4" tubing. I used smaller tubing for other vents on the roofs. I cut the Toy Shoppe kit chimney in half and used one part on the two buildings between the Java Huts. I made a new cap and inserted a piece of 3/16" tubing on top.

SOME EDGY BUSINESS

One bit of detail that is definitely worth mentioning is fixing the edges of the walls. The edges do not have any brick pattern on them; they are perfectly smooth. To fix this oversight I took my razor saw and sawed grooves in these edges to match the grooves between the bricks similar to the flat surface of the walls. My grooves were by no means perfect, but they looked much better than none at all.

Fig. 3-15. The side view of the Toy Shoppe part of the block. This shows the added bay, stairs, side door, the wider sidewalk, and Acme Realty, the seventh store. This store has Venetian blinds and one ply of facial tissue bonded behind the glass of the upper windows to give them a "frosted" look. This cornice is simpler than the one on the bakery.

Fig. 3-16. The first four stores expanded from two Java Huts.

with the roof slope, thus eliminating the stair-step look of the Java Hut. I capped these angled sides with strip stock as well. I also removed the mullions from the bottom of the three second-story front windows, converting them from 4 over 4 panes to 4 over 1. By now you have recognized that I have added different signs to the buildings, but I still refer to the kit name with which I began.

I haven't forgotten the kit door from which I cut the transom. I added this door to the side wall beneath the stairs by cutting an appropriate opening for it.

PAINTING AND WEATHERING

There was little painting left except for the roofs, which I made grimy black, and the concrete sidewalks and chimney caps, which I painted antique white. I painted the stacks and vents black. I also painted the bay window and outside stairway roofs grimy black. I left the outside stairway the white of the plastic since all the windows and doors in this kit were white to begin with. In most cases, I painted the Grandt Line doors the color of the rest of the building trim.

I painted some of the red brick walls with a white water-based paint wash. I used some signs provided as decals in the kits and made some on my computer.

Weathering is minimal as well. I used a wash made of India ink in alcohol to tone down everything a bit, with a spray of

Fig. 3-17. The right part of the four-store part of the block. I covered the hole in the side wall with .020 sheet and made it look like the remnant of a building that had been torn down. I hid it, even though I could have left this open because it will be covered by the other building.

Fig. 3-18. The rear of the block is plain but has a charm of its own. Note that the bakery is not only just a single story; it is not as deep as the buildings that flank it.

Testor's Dullcote for good measure. If a part of the interior could be seen through a window, like the white bracing or gray bases, I painted it flat black. After weathering, I snapped in the window glass and bonded it as well.

INTERIORS AND WINDOWS

Oh my, all those huge windows! How do I hide the emptiness inside? Well, first I took care of the smaller windows by placing shades and curtains in most of them. The shades are paper bonded to the back of the glass, which I had put in place after weathering. I drew the curtains on white paper with water-based felt-tipped markers. I overlapped each stroke, which produced a rippled effect. You can bond the shades and curtains to the glass with the liquid styrene solvent by brushing it on the paper from the back.

The large storefront windows still presented a problem, however. I added curtains in some of these, and Venetian blinds, as described in Chapter 1, in others. I blocked off the three upper storefront windows in a few or at least made them translucent by painting them with the solvent on the inside. One has the sign covering the upper windows. But store windows are purposely large to show off the wares of the merchant who owns the store, so in a few windows I added a shelf behind the glass and placed all kinds of odds and ends from my scrap box on the shelf. Most were painted bright colors. I added a ½"-high back to the shelves, which helped hide the interiors some more. I leave the rest to you.

CONCLUSION

Making this block shows how doodles help you plan what you want to build. What I have described in the last three chapters is how to execute doodles. I used three kits and wound up with seven stores (rather economical, I might add). You can add a third story to either end building by getting another kit.

You may recall that I once mentioned that there were too many "city buildings" available, but I could not resist using the new Walthers kits because they are so well thought out. I also made the Toy Shoppe as different from a stock kit as possible. In this project the possibilities are easy to develop with simple, and practical, doodling.

Note that as you worked through each of the last three chapters, the degree of difficulty increased a bit, and hopefully, so did your confidence. Many of the techniques I mentioned in these doodling chapters will come in handy as you work through subsequent chapters, so you may want to refer to them often.

The simple station basically uses the main two-story part of one kit plus the end wall from a second kit. The freighthouse in the background utilizes most of the rest. I patched the area in which the tower originally sat with wooden shingles.

This is the Rico station that everyone else has, right out of the box, including the tower.

4 Three Rico Stations

The real Rico station is on the Rio Grande Southern, a narrow gauge railroad in the Colorado Rocky Mountains. This station is typical, with a passenger section and an attached freighthouse. There is even space on the second floor for the agent to live or for additional railroad offices.

The Lionel Rico station kit is highly recognizable and you'd probably find it on more layouts than any other plastic station. If you have one already, you're already familiar with how it is built. If this is your first station, you will now see how to go beyond the kit's instructions to build a more personalized version. In this chapter we will build three small stations, plus a freighthouse, from the parts in three station kits.

STATION NUMBER ONE: THE EASY STATION

The first station I will show you how to build is a smaller, simpler version of the

Fig. 4-1. The Rico-Wrongo is almost a mirror image of the original Rico kit.

Fig. 4-2. This shows Rico-Wrongo from the rear.

Rico station. This station uses all of the parts from one Rico station kit except those for the freighthouse and the main wall where the freighthouse is attached to the passenger area. To begin I assembled the passenger portion following the kit instructions. When it came time to add the last wall that adjoins the freighthouse, I substituted the windowed wall from a second station; the two are exactly the same size. By using the main station parts from one kit plus a single wall from a second kit, I turned two kits into one station.

That's almost all there was to it, other than the addition of detail. Other things you can do include adding interior braces in all corners using small pieces of 1/8" and 3/16" square Evergreen strip styrene. This is for the extra strength they provide and to aid in keeping the corners square. I used similar braces in every joint. Some braces are smaller sizes. For example, .060 strips are a good choice in the agent's bay window, where the larger braces will not fit. Use similar braces to attach the roofs to the walls, the walls to the base, and in the joint at the peak of the roof.

There is one distinctive feature on the Rico kits that I also changed: the odd tower on the right side of the front roof peak. I say "odd" because almost none of the other Rio Grande Southern stations had such a tower, and in later years it was even removed from this station. Every once in a while a manufacturer makes a model with a prototype feature that might make it more distinctive, but in the long run it becomes apparent that the kit would have had a more universal appeal if the feature had been left off. So off went the tower.

THREE WAYS TO REPAIR A ROOF

Eliminating the tower caused a problem: How was I to get rid of the blank area in the shingled roof where the tower was supposed to have been attached? I could use the rear roof peak, with a smaller bare

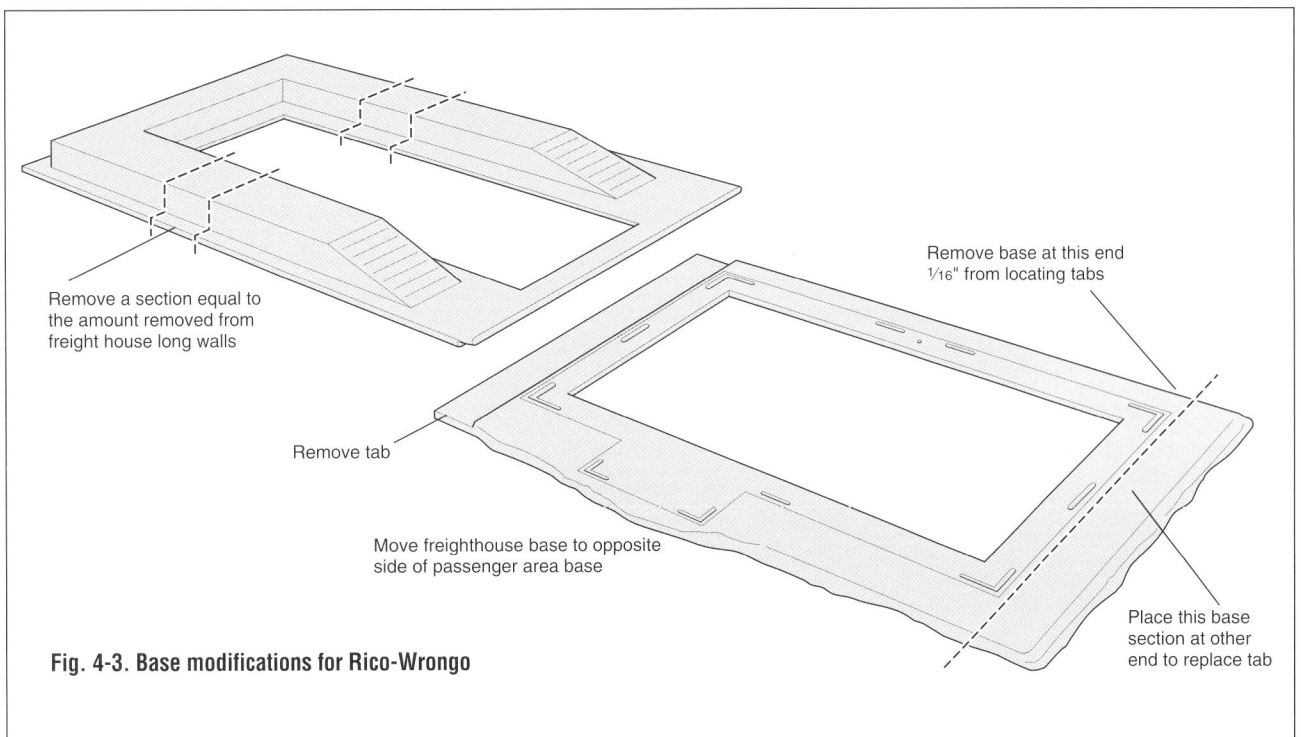

Fig. 4-3. Base modifications for Rico-Wrongo

area where the chimney is supposed to go, from the second kit, and trade it for the roof on the front where the tower was supposed to be. That's one way, and a very simple fix. However, this would put a chimney on the front and I thought it was a bad architectural choice; it just didn't look right with a chimney there. (As a matter of fact, this roof part has the chimney right over a window which isn't right anyway. All the more reason to do something else to correct my problem.)

A second way to repair the roof is to cut out the bare areas from the roof pieces and replace the resulting holes with small pieces of matching shingle cut from the tower pieces or from another roof piece. This isn't too hard to do, especially since the shingles have a rough pattern that tends to hide most discrepancies. When I cut out the larger bare area, I wound up with just a top triangle and a bottom triangle; the bare area goes all the way to the angled edge and in cutting it out I went right to the edge. The addition of the shingle patch got the roof back to its original size. All these patching methods require careful measuring and cutting and then careful filing to get things to fit without any gaps. I added bracing using small pieces of scrap sheet styrene across all joints on the back. Do not place any bracing where the roofs will be attached to the peaked wall tops.

The third repair method involves leaving all roof pieces where they belong, with no substitutions, and treating the large bare area as if it were a real patch in the shingle roof. However, this patch must look as if it were applied on top of the existing shingles, so the patch must be higher than the tops of the shingles alongside it.

I used a piece of thin black plastic from the flower trays my wife bought at a garden center. I washed the trays, and then cut out all the flat side areas. I cut a patch to the size of the bare area and bonded this in place. It took two identical pieces, placed one on top of the other, to gain the necessary thickness. I scribed a few lines across this patch to represent seams of a tarpaper-covered patch. If you think this patch might stand out too much, go back to the first method. I made the first two types of repairs and I used them on two stations. I placed the best-looking ones on the front peak. I added the chimneys and trim, and, bingo! I had my basic smaller Rico station.

Did I accomplish what I started out to do? Yes, I think I improved the look of my station, and each option was worth the extra effort. You may not feel this way, so

Fig. 4-4. The smaller station lacks the upper floors and has a new end wall. I scribed the shortened loading platform and painted it to look like wood.

Fig. 4-5. This view shows the smaller station and the scribed platforms from the rear.

leaving the tower in place would certainly make this the simplest kitmingle of all.

STATION NUMBER TWO: RICO-WRONGO

The plans that appeared in the October 1962 issue of *Model Railroader* magazine are the plans on which the Lionel station was based. The real Rico was 108 feet long and Lionel shortened their kit to 80 feet and simplified it somewhat. Let's assume you already have the original non-kitmingled Rico station on your railroad. You also have the smaller one we just made. Now, just to be different, how about making something the "wrong way," as far as everybody else's Rico station is concerned?

Well, that's what I did, and it's relatively easy. Even though I had almost a complete set of parts left over from the second Rico kit, I chose to begin with a third, brand-new Rico kit. I also decided to place the freighthouse on the opposite end from where it was supposed to go on the Lionel version. In order to move the freighthouse, I assembled the passenger area with the two end walls swapped.

But first I had another choice to make. I could make a longer freighthouse since I had the parts from three kits, or I could make it smaller. I chose to make it smaller even though the real Rico station had a 70-foot-long freighthouse. You might choose either option, but the space you have available on your layout may be the deciding factor. (I have a third station and a separate freighthouse to tell you about later in this chapter, so if you choose to make a longer freighthouse, it will affect the next two buildings.) Later you will find out later why I chose to make the freighthouse shorter.

In either case, the procedure for building the freighthouse is the same. I had to cut the side walls and the roofs apart and splice them back together again. I cut two sections from each side wall 2 3/16" wide, and then put the walls back together again with braces inside at the joint. (The reason for this precise length will become very apparent when I get to the freighthouse.) I also cut 2³⁄₁₆" from the ends of both roof pieces so they would fit the shortened freighthouse. I added the shortened freighthouse to the rest of the station, thus creating Rico-Wrongo.

THE FOUNDATION FOR IT ALL

I have not mentioned much about the bases supplied with the Rico kits, so you might have assumed that I used all of them according to the instructions. Wrong. I modified the base for the second station because it went the wrong way. I had to cut off the tab that connected the two base sections and cut off the base on the opposite side. I bonded this base part to the other side to replace the tab I had just removed. This base-adjusting allowed me to attach the freighthouse base part on the "wrong end." (See fig. 4-3 for the way I altered the bases.)

You'll note that I also did something different to the base of the first station. Here I made cuts about ¹⁄₁₆" out from the wall-locating tabs cast into the bases and removed the outer part of the base. This is an extra step, but when it was done, the base looked like a concrete foundation. It is one of the most difficult procedures of these kitmingles: the difficulty is that these bases are so thick (more than ⅛") that it takes a while to cut through them.

On the second station, I scribed the platform sides to make them look like wood. I scribed horizontal boards on the sides of the platform rather than using the cast stone supplied in the kits. I thought this would be a nice variation from the stone. To do this I made a guide from a small scrap of styrene and sawed three slits into the end. Each slit was at the height where I wanted to scribe a horizontal line. Then I used this to guide my knife horizontally along the sides. I put the tip of my knife into a slit where I wanted a line and I moved the guide along with the knife so the line was always the same height. I slid the guide along with its bottom resting on the platform base. I used the triangular stone piece as a guide at the sloped ramp edge. I also added a few vertical board ends and a couple of cracks and broken boards. I then scribed some wood grain on the boards with my knife.

Fig. 4-6. Wall construction

On the third station, described shortly, I scribed some of the flat base areas so they looked like partial board platforms, filing these areas smooth and removing the bumpy texture prior to scribing the boards. I cut off all angled edges of the bases as well. Last, I cut and spliced the freighthouse platforms to match the new length of my shorter version of the freighthouses.

STATION NUMBER THREE: THE UNRICOGNIZABLE RICO

The third station is the most difficult and also the most different, yet it will

Fig. 4-7. The Real Rico station. The Lionel version follows it closely but not exactly. They shortened the freighthouse and the main passenger area. Prototype photo.

Fig. 4-8. The plans show that the peaks in the front and rear roof have been centered and the area where the freighthouse joins the passenger portion has been modified. Prototype plans.

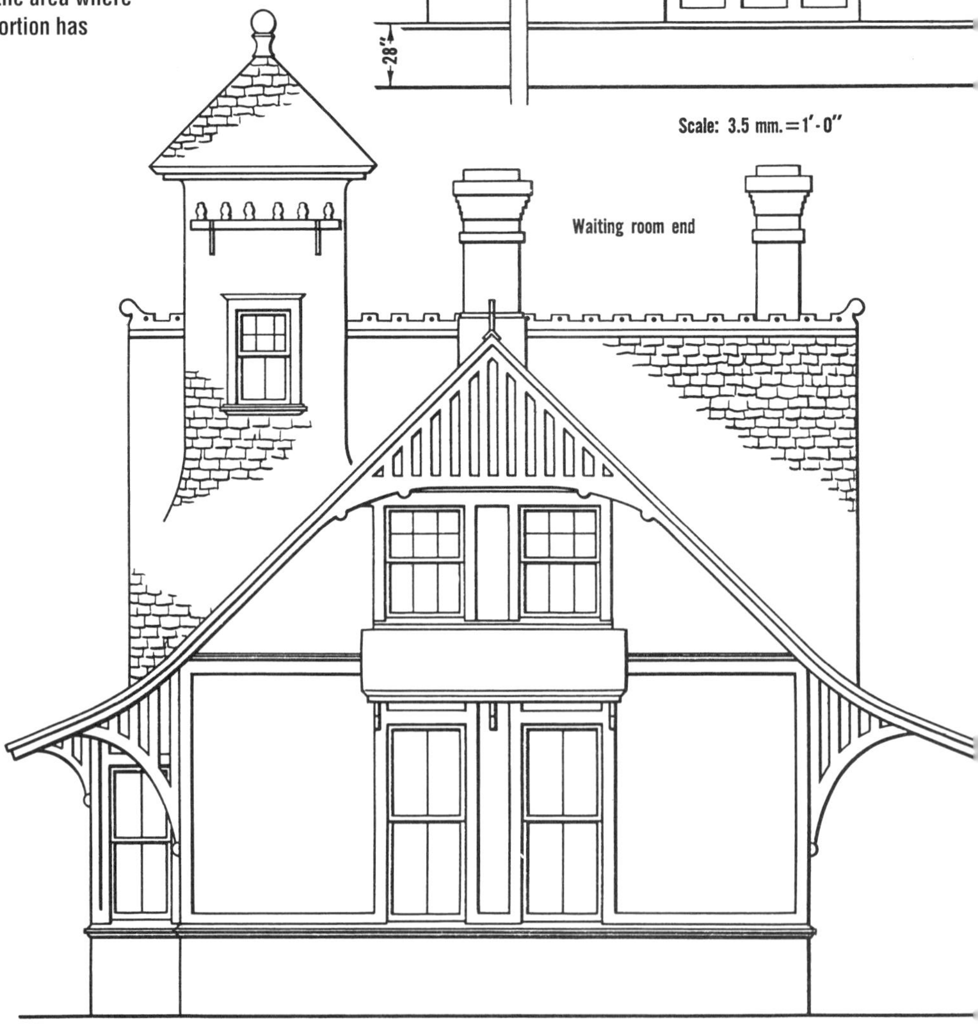

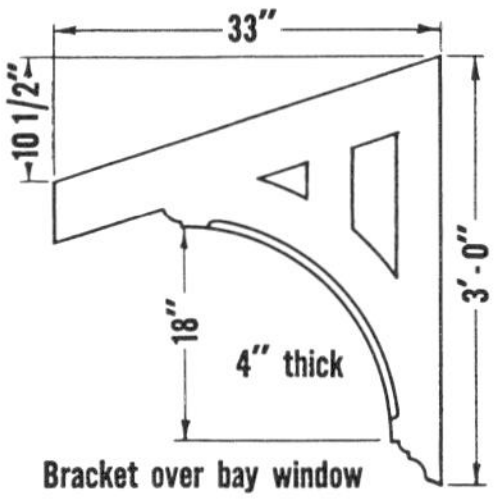

Drawn for MODEL RAILROADER MAGAZINE by
ROBERT WEGNER
Plans in MODEL RAILROADER may be photocopied for noncommercial use only.

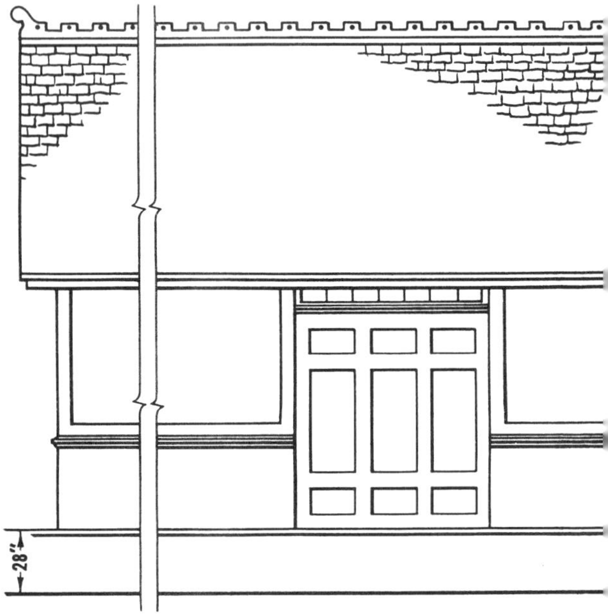

Scale: 3.5 mm. = 1'-0"

Waiting room end

Bracket over bay window

3/8" = 1'-0"

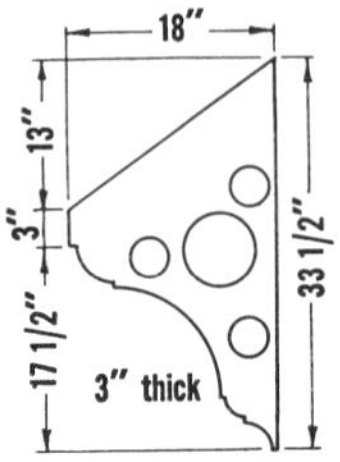

Bracket for projection over windows of waiting room

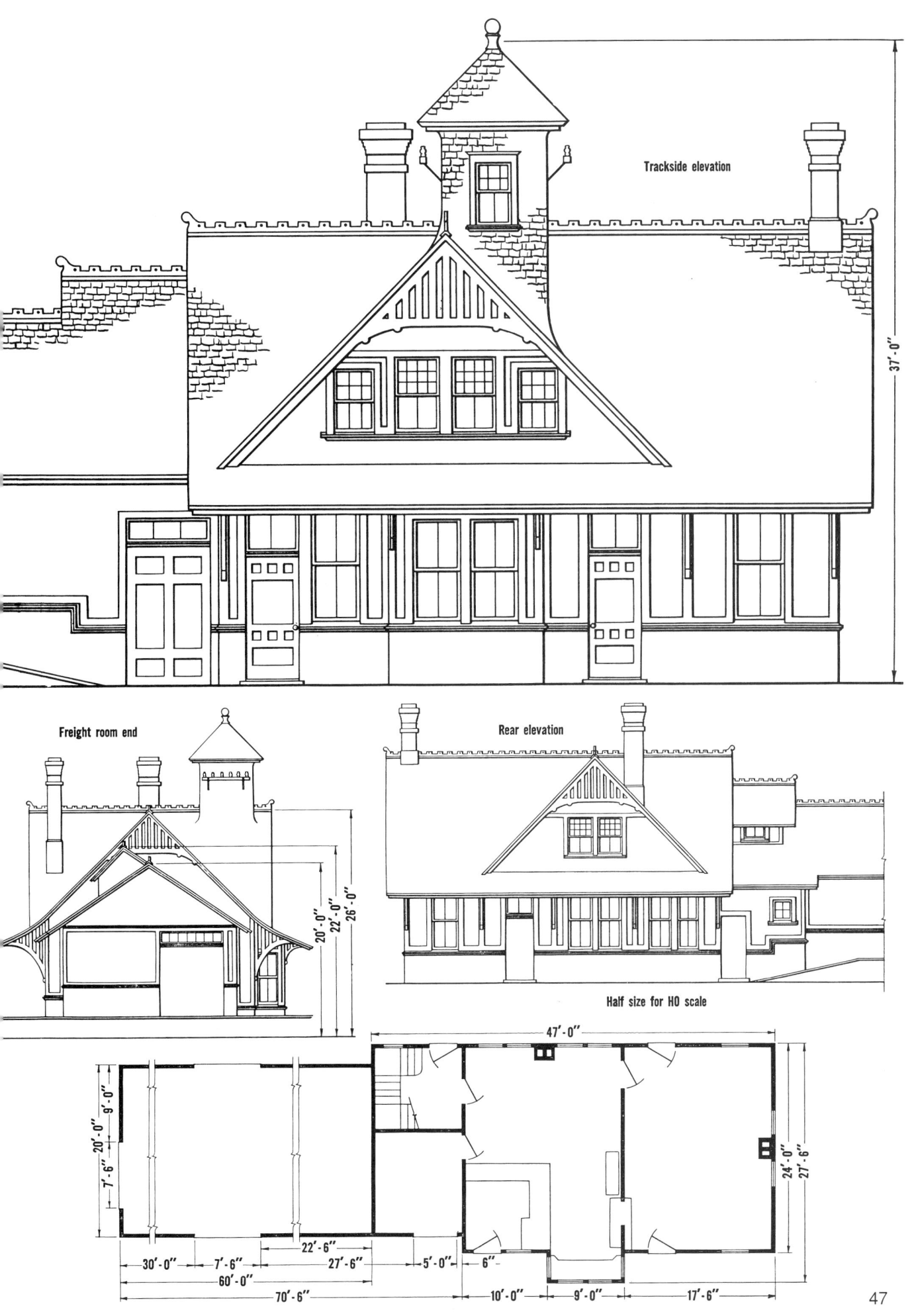

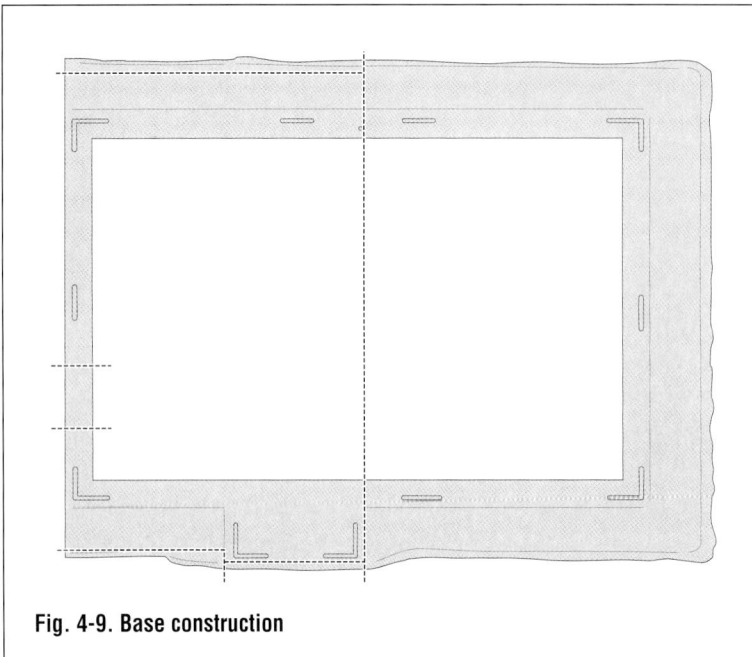

Fig. 4-9. Base construction

with the exception of a peak for the last one. I went to the remaining parts from the first kit and removed the peak from that kit's freighthouse end wall. I bonded this atop my new end wall. I could now assemble all four walls together on this low station.

I had four freighthouse roof pieces left, so I cut two segments 5" long from one piece and bonded each to a full-length piece to make two long roofs. I filed each mating end smooth and added braces across the back of the joints as I always do.

Next, I assembled the agent's bay and added that to the front wall. I then noted the angle of the new roof and found that I had to cut down the tops of the bay sides and the bay front, since these walls had to be lower than they were on the stock kit. I also measured where the new front roof would go over the bay and placed a roof extension over the bay. I used the small roof that was supposed to go over the end windows on the main station end walls. (I did not use these small roofs on any of my new stations.) I cut off the back edge of this small roof and bonded the larger part to the long roof over the bay.

The roof is rather long, so I made a center support by tracing the end roof peak angles onto a piece of .040 sheet and added this support in the middle of the long walls. Next, I added the doors and windows and then bonded the new roofs in place. I modified the bases to fit the new wall size. The freighthouse portion was used "as is" with the exception of shortening it to match the shortened front and back walls. I also cut away much of the base material from the low station, including that around the edges of the platform. I cut the remaining base in three places to make it fit the shorter and narrower passenger area. (See fig. 4-9, which also shows where I cut the base down.)

A NEW FREIGHTHOUSE

I still had a complete set of freighthouse parts, which were enough to make a small separate freighthouse that could be used with any station. I also had the two 2 3/16"-wide wall pieces from the second station freighthouse. (I also had a small piece of the rear passenger area wall that I had never used.)

I made vertical cuts in both long walls at the point where the angle for the platform

retain the family look since it is made from the same kit. I made this station a much lower one by eliminating the second floor that the others have, and this one is only as wide as the freighthouse portion. The first thing I did was cut off the peaked portions of the front and back passenger area walls. This cut is at a point that will match the height of the lower freighthouse walls. Figure 4-6 shows where I made the cuts in these walls.

I also cut a segment 1" wide out of each freighthouse side wall. I had one bad window casting in one kit and therefore had to find a way to cover this opening. I planned to use this extra wall material to fill in the window opening. If you're lucky, you won't have to do this, but I wanted to show you that there is always a way to get around a problem.

In fig. 4-6 you can also see where I made three vertical cuts. I attached the part of the front wall, with the agent's bay, to the front of the freighthouse wall. I then attached the double-windowed part of the rear wall to the corresponding freighthouse wall. This gave me the front and back walls of this station and I used the freighthouse end wall "as is." To make the other end wall, I took the right half of the front wall and bonded the small end segment of the kit's rear wall to it. I did this so there would always be vertical trim at all corners. Now I had all four walls begins (see fig. 4-10). I filed these edges smooth and added the two small 2³⁄₁₆" segments to their respective walls at the new edge. Note that I say "respective," because they are not the same.

To make the one remaining end wall, I used the two ends I had just cut off the long walls. I joined them door to door and then trimmed off the ends so this wall was 5" wide. Then I scraped away both angled boards on this end wall and scribed in new vertical boards below the angled area. These continued the boards already there. I also scribed in new vertical boards on the two bare areas of the new segments just added to the long walls. This is the area below the horizontal board at the bottom of the wainscoting.

Next, I had to make 45-degree angles on the edges of these walls. See Chapter 2 for instructions.

I bonded all four walls together with the appropriate bracing, and then began to modify the base with the platforms. I cut off the base across a line at the end of the ramps. Then I used one of the base ends I had cut from the first station to span the gap. I needed to rest the new end wall on this. I cut two notches in the ends so the base would be set back from the ramp ends, which are even with the end wall (see fig. 4-11). I bonded this base in place and then added the four walls to the new base.

FLAT ROOF OR PEAKED ROOF?

My walls were even at the top, so the easiest roof to add was a flat one. If your layout is in a warmer climate, you can try this; however, if your station has to withstand Colorado-type winters, it certainly needs a peaked roof to shed the snow.

I had already used the top of the peaked end wall on the low station, but remember that I still had the two walls left that connected the passenger area to the freighthouse portion of Rico. These came to my rescue. I cut two triangular peaked segments from one of these to fit on my end walls (see fig. 4-12). I scribed the bare area vertically with spacing about the same as on the wainscoting. It was easy to get the right roof pitch by cutting along the lower edge of the raised part that was supposed to support the freighthouse roof if it were joined as intended. I cut the peak horizontally at the bottom and used the first peak as a template to cut the second one. I added these to the end walls.

I had one full freighthouse roof piece left over plus two main roof pieces. I also had the two 2³⁄₁₆" pieces I cut from the shortened roofs of the "wrong way" station. I cut across the two main station roofs to match the height of the freighthouse roof. Then I cut off the ends vertically as close as possible to the center openings. This

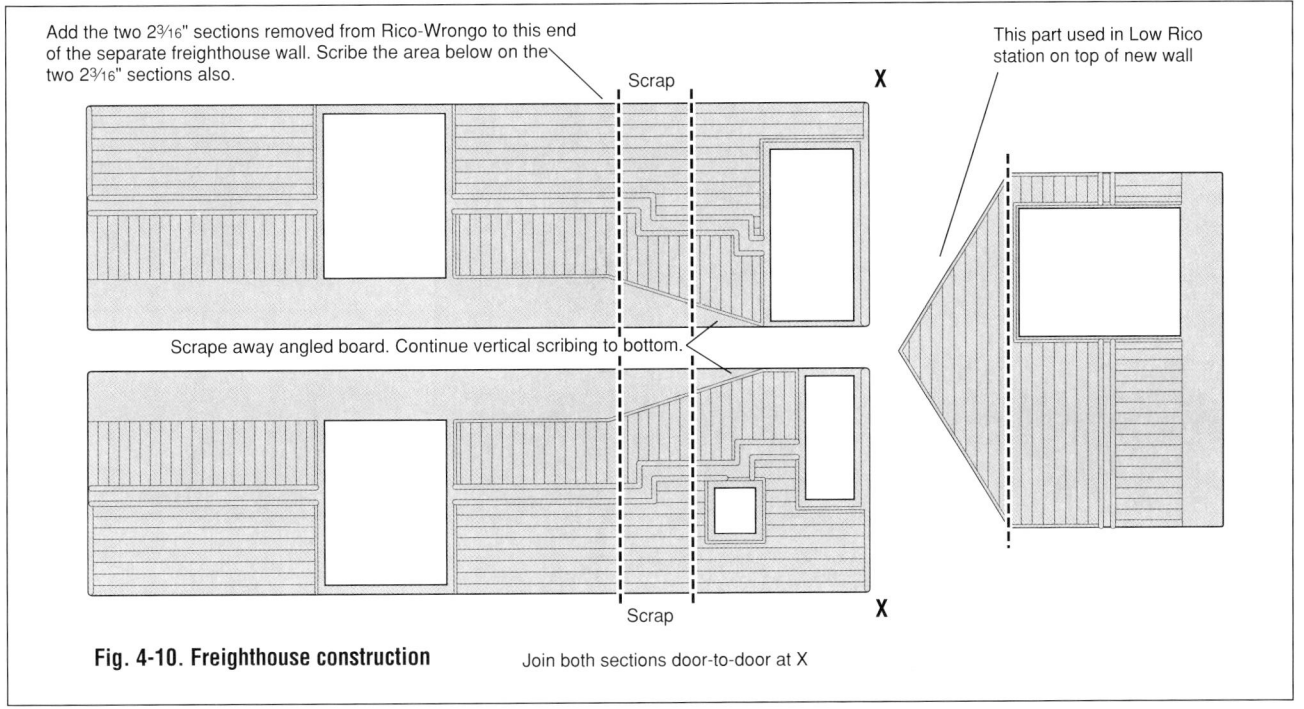

Fig. 4-10. Freighthouse construction Join both sections door-to-door at X

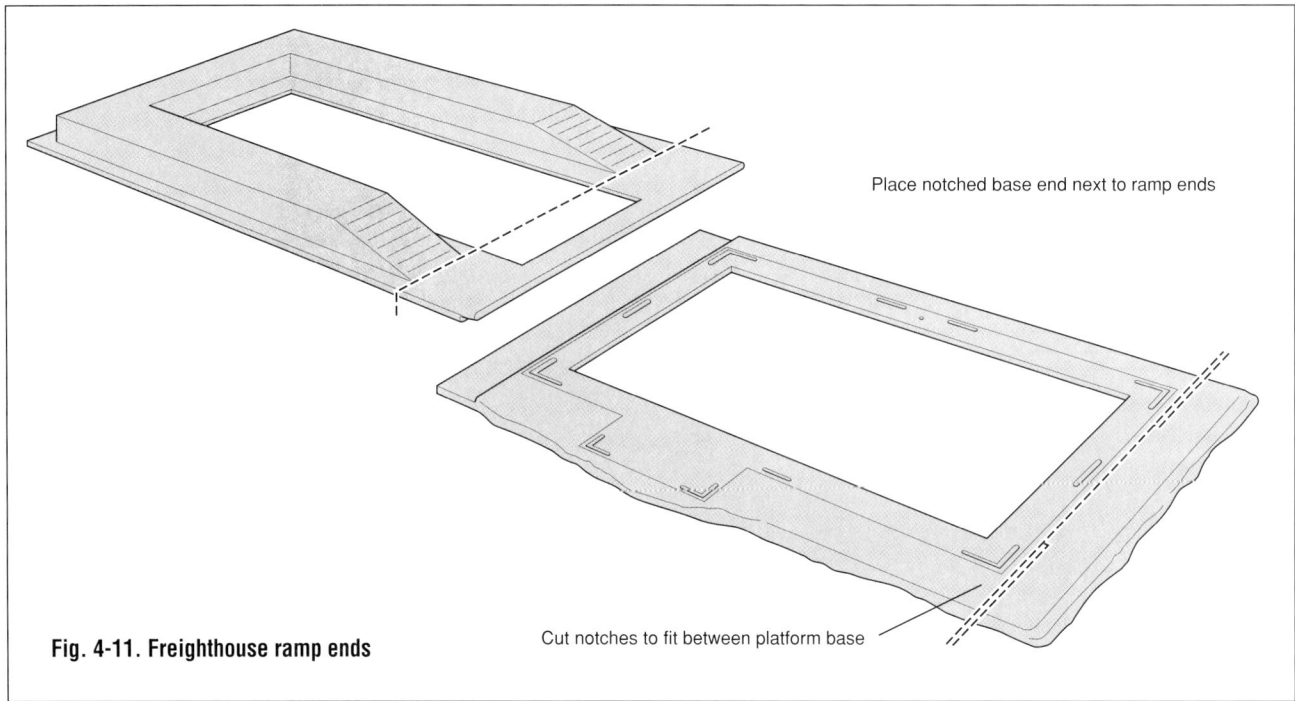

Fig. 4-11. Freighthouse ramp ends

Place notched base end next to ramp ends

Cut notches to fit between platform base

gave me four roof segments 2⅝" wide. I spliced these together with one of the smaller 2³⁄₁₆" segments in the center. As it turned out, I had to cut down this smaller segment to be 1" in width. This made the spliced roof the same length as the full-sized one. I placed the spliced roof on the back part of the freighthouse.

If you're not a big fan of cutting and splicing, one option would be to cut two rectangular roof pieces, the same size as the one full freighthouse roof, from .060 sheet stock. Bond these in place on the new end peaks. To make this look like rolled roofing, place a single ply of facial tissue on the roof and paint through it with Floquil grimy black. The paint bonds the tissue to the roof. When it's dry, trim off the ends and add tar joints with a black felt-tipped pen and a ruler to guide it. This simpler roof replaces the shingled roof, which you can salt away for use another time.

Next, I added the doors, the one window, and a smokestack made from a piece of round sprue (also called a runner). That completed the freight station.

MAKING THE STATIONS UNIQUE

I modified the chimneys by filing the bottom angles so they were smooth and then I joined the angled bottoms together. I waited overnight for this bond to solidify and then cut the bases apart in the middle. This gave each chimney a flat bottom rather than an angled one. Then I cut openings in the roof peaks and inserted the chimneys in the openings. This way I avoided a chimney being behind a window, as I mentioned earlier. This station also has a scribed freight platform.

WASTE NOT, WANT NOT

I don't like to waste any material that I remove, so I made a small coal box from leftovers and added it to the end of the Rico-Wrongo. I made it from the leftover wainscoting I had removed from the low station and the freighthouse. By placing the coal box on the end where I had added the base, I provided additional bracing to secure this base to the wall of the station.

I added a small extension at one end of the freighthouse platform by utilizing two of the small segments I had removed when shortening the other platforms. I bonded two similar widths together (the front and back platforms are different) and placed them against the platform. I removed a portion of the base to allow the extension to abut the main platform. Then I added some of the leftover stone pieces to the sides and across the end.

So far my aim had been to give all of the stations a common look. However, the other definition of kitmingling is to make things look different, so I made a different kind of gable trim on the first station than that supplied in the Lionel kits. (You could omit all trim, which would also alter the look, although it would be rather plain.)

I made a simpler trim by sawing off the curved lower part of the gable trim and bonding a portion of the upper track of the freighthouse door horizontally across the bottom. (I bonded my freight doors permanently in place so I did not need the tracks.) The real Rico trim was not curved at the bottom, so this new trim is actually more authentic. Figure 4-13 shows how and also shows the chimney modification and the scribing guide.

The first station also received a passenger platform and an added roof extension to provide some extra shelter for passengers waiting for a train. I made the platform from pieces of .080 sheet and added these to the bottom of the trimmed-down base. I then added .100 x .188 strips underneath, around the perimeter of the platform, even with the outer edges. This platform raised the station about ¼". As a matter of fact, I suggest that all the stations be placed on a ¼" piece of plywood or foamboard to raise them. This is because the Rico station was on a narrow gauge railroad and the loading ramps are therefore lower than on standard gauge railroads. Raising everything ¼" places the platforms closer to standard gauge height.

To make the roof extension, I cut out the center area from the two main roofs that I had already chopped up to get the parts for the freighthouse roof. I used the full width below the opening in this main roof for the rear part of the extension and cut out a small piece from the front portion that abuts the curved edge of the main station roof. This allowed me to place the rear of the roof extension against the station side wall. I bonded the two roof sections together at the peak and added some ⅛" braces at the joint. To support the extension, I bonded two of the larger door tracks back to back, forming a T-shaped post. Then I cut off the top of one end of the post that matched the V of the underside of the peak. Next, I bonded two leftover roof braces to the top of the post, one on each side, against the bottom leg of the T and against the underside of the T

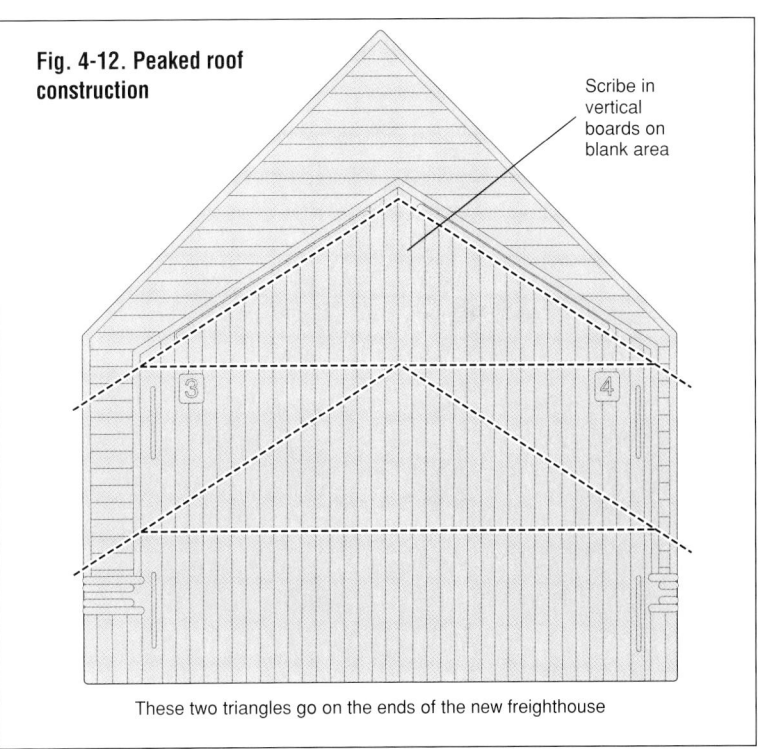

Fig. 4-12. Peaked roof construction

Scribe in vertical boards on blank area

These two triangles go on the ends of the new freighthouse

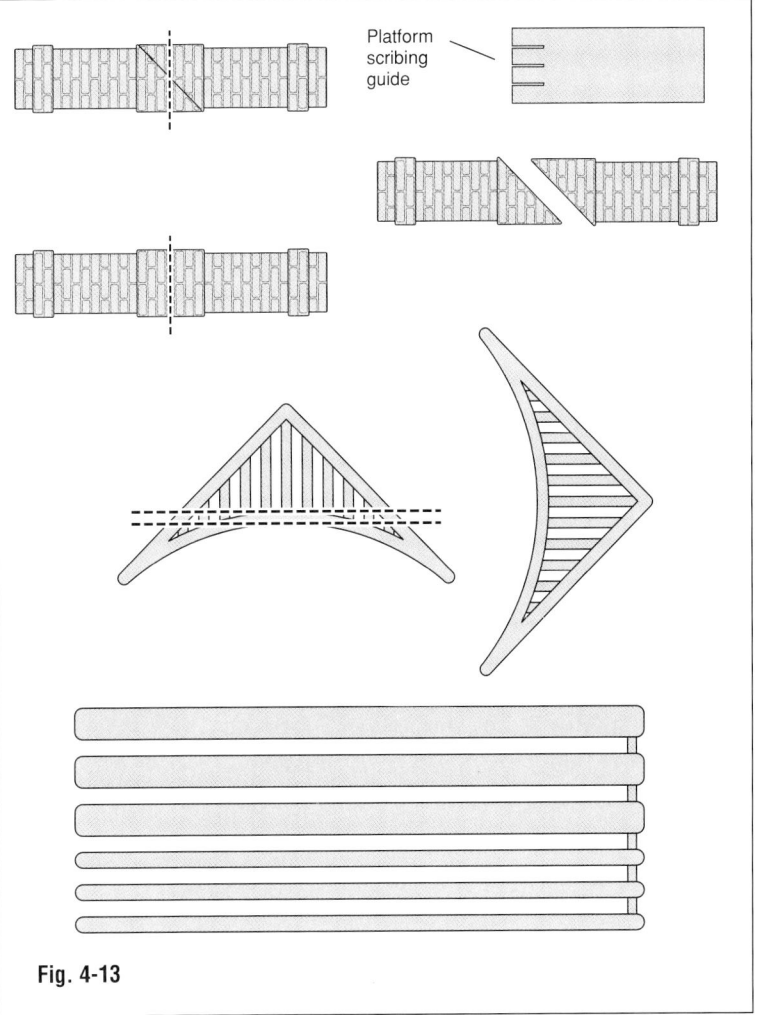

Platform scribing guide

Fig. 4-13

Fig. 4-14. The freighthouse is a good companion for the simple station since that now lacks the freight area.

tops. I filed down the straight edges of the brace a bit so they would match the curve of the roof better. This was a file-and-fit procedure until I got it to fit the underside of the roof (see fig. 4-16).

Next, I bonded the roof extension to the main roof. I added a small strip of .015 sheet, which I pre-curved to the shape of the roof curve, to brace the underside of the adjoining roofs. I also added a 1/8" square strip brace at the joint of the main roof and the underside of the longer rear extension, since this is a 90-degree joint. With the extension bonded in place, I measured the distance between the extension roof peak and the platform and cut off the bottom of the post at this length. Then I bonded the post in place between the two. I added a second post in the center of the extension but without the braces at

Fig. 4-15. In this view you can see the basic freighthouse with no distractions.

the sides. This extension makes this station quite distinct but still a member of the family.

The bench on the platform is scratch-built and is there to provide some extra bracing between the two posts and the concrete base. I also included other roof patches on the station that already had two patches. By doing this, you make the required patches less obvious. I cut a rectangular hole in the roof and inserted a rectangular .080 sheet patch into it. Then I added the flower tray material on top. Simple? Easy? Yes!

A LITTLE PAINT GOES A LONG WAY

I did very little painting, preferring to keep the stations in the tan and brown colors in which they were molded. If your railroad has a special paint scheme for its buildings, you should of course use them on these stations.

My painting was more in the form of weathering. First I used Floquil roof brown diluted with Diosol, the thinner for Floquil paints, mixing one part paint with three parts thinner, creating a wash. I painted all of the roofs and wooden parts of the platforms with this wash. After this dried, I drybrushed Floquil Polly-S white on the roofs, using a ½"-wide stiff-bristled brush

Drybrushing is dipping the brush in paint, wiping almost all of it off on a paper towel or rag, and then brushing on the remaining paint. As its name implies, you are painting with a (relatively) "dry brush." Using a stiff-bristled brush helps to keep the paint out of the crevices and mostly on the raised portion of the shingles.

I used a black wash on the wooden platforms. This was an even thinner wash, made up of about fifteen parts water to one part Floquil Polly-S black paint.

I painted the concrete platform on station number one with Floquil antique white and the chimneys with Floquil S P scarlet. I painted the inside of the chimneys Floquil flat black. When all the paint was dry, I sprayed the entire building with Testor's Dullcote lacquer, which flattens the shine.

If this is your first attempt at weathering, there are plenty of small scrap pieces left over so you can practice these painting techniques on them to get the feeling and to see the results beforehand.

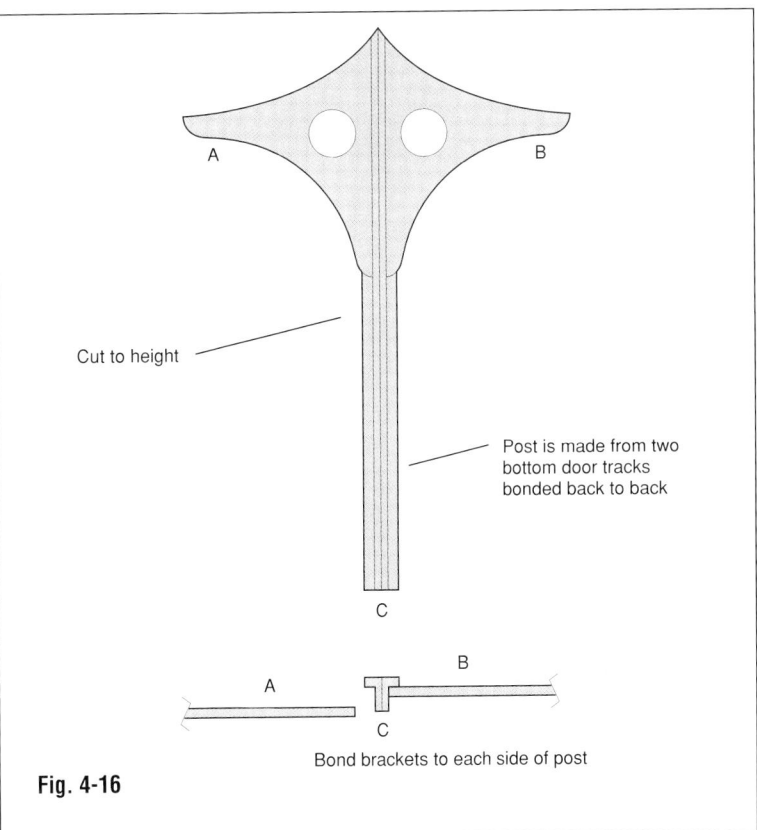

Fig. 4-16

DOING WINDOWS

There is no "glass" in these kits, so I used .015 clear Evergreen styrene pieces bonded to the walls behind all windows and doors. I added some shades cut from light, buff-colored typing paper on most windows. I bonded these to the windows by placing the shades where I wanted them and flowed solvent on the back of the shades. The paper acts like a blotter and the solvent goes right through the shade to the styrene glass and secures it. I varied the height of the shades by using different lengths of paper.

HINDSIGHT IS ALWAYS 20/20

After completing the Rico-Wrongo, it dawned on me that I could have made it much more easily if I had merely swapped the front and back passenger area walls and kept the bases and everything else intact. The only thing that would have to be adjusted was the base so that the agent's bay would have a place to rest. I could have cut off this base area and swapped this also. There would have been some adjustments in doing this, such as removing some base wall locating tabs, for instance, but it probably would have been

WARNING: KIT IN BOX

I encountered some problems with this kit and other kits used throughout this book. Look for them before you begin so there will be no surprises. For instance, in this kit about half of the window openings are off center. To fix this, file or scrape some plastic off the edge toward which the window must move in order to be centered. Also, watch for bumps on the ends of walls with 45-degree bevels molded into them. File these bumps flat. Other areas where you cut off a part of the sprue may have a bump. File it smooth so there will be a good bonding surface. If you don't, only the bump will bond, since the area around it will not touch the piece with which it is trying to join.

Often the corner angles are not truly 45 degrees, which is why I so emphatically recommend adding square strip bracing in all corners.

When using plans or diagrams always measure on your model or the part referred to. Many plans and diagrams are not totally accurate, so the best way is to actually check the parts with which you are working for final sizes.

Another thing never mentioned in the instructions is that you have to file the peaks of the roofs flat so the fancy trim can bond there. The trim pieces also have an angle on the bottom and you need to file these flat, too. All kit parts must have an angle on some edges in order to be released from the mold, so be aware of this.

I sometimes think many kit designers never had to put a kit together, which results in some ill-fitting parts and poor design. In the above examples, the fact that the instructions don't tell us about the peaks or the angles is disturbing. Some kit instructions do, and that's nice. However, they make it seem so simple, never cautioning you that there may be some pitfalls or special precautions you must take in order to assemble the kit successfully. In most cases I will clue you in to a problem and give you my solution. Even if you do not use it here, it may prove valuable on some other kit you may assemble in the future.

---

easier than the way I actually did it. I'm sorry I didn't think of this earlier, but I sometimes do things the first way that pops into my head. Most often I'm right, but this time hindsight seems to be communicating a better way.

BEATING THE AUTHOR AT HIS OWN GAME

As you read this chapter, you may see variations beyond those I made (and I hope you do). One example might be to cut off the front peak from one of the stations that has a second floor and replace it with the rear peak from the unused top of the low station. This would give the front a slightly different appearance: two windows rather than four.

If you do not want to make a separate freighthouse, you can utilize the one wall segment I did not use from the low station and really shorten one of the long freighthouse walls. By adding this segment to the shortened long wall, you would wind up with a very small combination station without an agent's bay. The long wall could be shortened a lot by eliminating the large freight door altogether, since there is still the door on the end wall for handling freight. And since I'm making wishes, I wish I had made my low station much shorter by removing 3" rather than 1" from the freighthouse walls. I am sure by now you can envision many more options beyond those I've shown, such as adding a baggage door to the first station somewhere on an end wall.

CONCLUSION

I made all of my versions smaller than the original. It seems obvious that I could have combined two Ricos and made a much larger station with or without freighthouses. If I had made the Rico without a freighthouse, I could have made a double-sized stand-alone freighthouse. I have seen many versions in which this has been accomplished very successfully. Now that I have shared with you all of the techniques needed for you to make a larger station, I hope you will be encouraged to do as I say, not as I do.

The gates are controlled from this tower, the height of which provides the watchman with a good view up and down the track.

This interlocking tower yielded the parts for the yard office and elevated grade crossing shanty.

5 A Yard Office and an Elevated Grade Crossing Shanty

Every railroad needs a yard office, a few grade crossing shanties, and interlocking towers. Most of you have a Plasticville interlocking tower. It's been around since 1952, so there must be thousands of layouts that have one with brown or gray walls and the opposite colors for the roof, stairs, and doors. In this chapter, I'll show you how to give this building new life by turning it into two different buildings, a yard office and an elevated grade crossing shanty. One is very

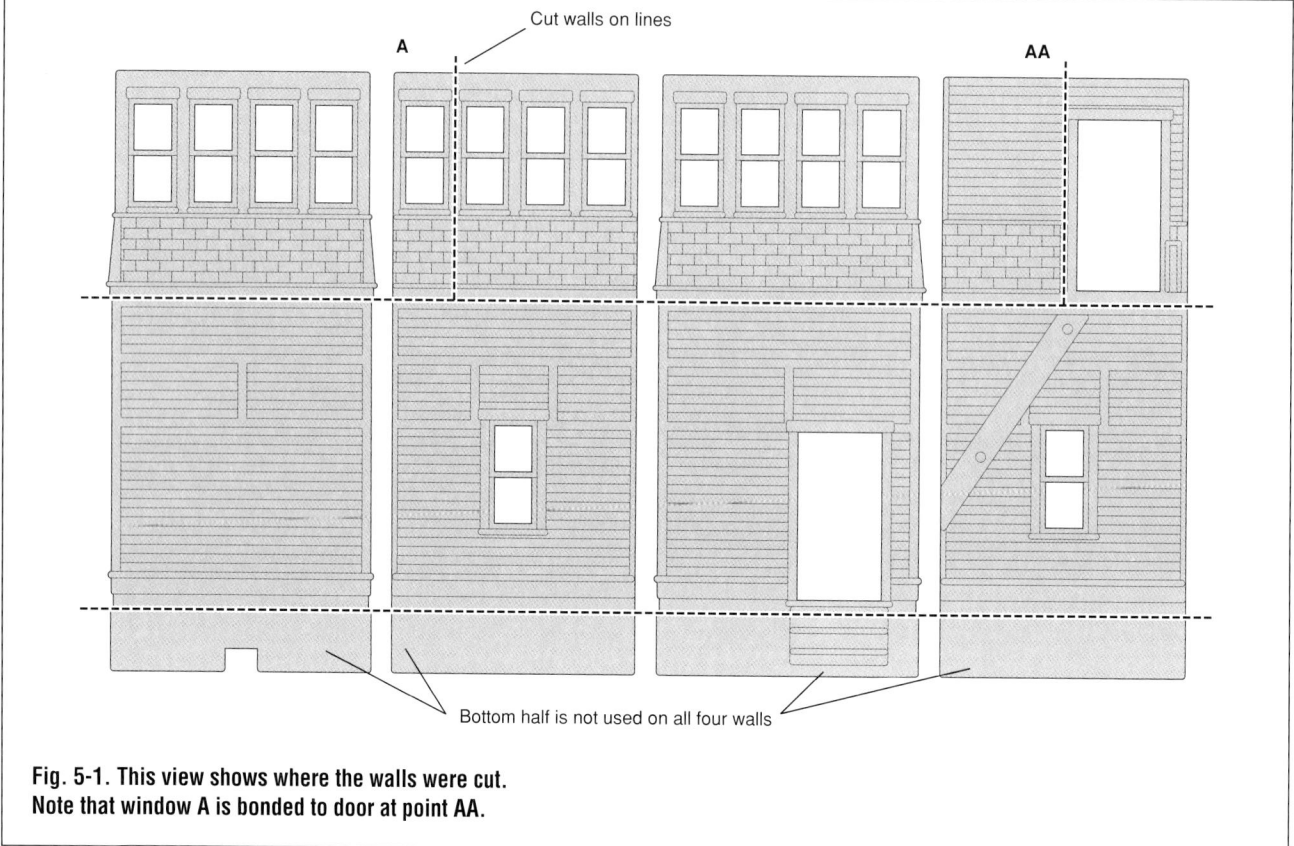

Fig. 5-1. This view shows where the walls were cut. Note that window A is bonded to door at point AA.

simple and the other is as complex as you want to make it.

THE SIMPLE YARD OFFICE

To make the yard office, I sawed off each wall at the second ridge below the shingled top area. (Figure 5-1 shows where I made these saw cuts.) Next I sawed off the bottom above the ½" base of the building.

I bonded these walls using the interlocking tabs to line up things correctly. Next, I added the roof, smokestack, and door. There are eight round projections on the underside of the roof that hold the roof in place. I had to shave a little off of the inner side of each with a chisel blade in order to get the projections to fit over the side walls. Once I was satisfied that the roof would fit, I filed a small bevel on all top edges of the walls so there would be more surface touching the underside of the roof (this made bonding easier). Then I bonded the roof in place.

Last, I painted the walls to match the Rico stations: brown for the door and black for the roof. I used a special mixture for the walls, which I could cover later. All that was left was to bond Evergreen .010 clear styrene rectangles behind the windows.

A FEW TRICKS

These Plasticville kits are made with a very brittle variation of plastic (don't drop it or try to bend it!). One of my windows had a big chunk missing in the window frame on the lower side. Rather than try to repair it, I filed away the remaining window and treated it as if it was open, so there is only glass in the upper window frame. I made a shelf beneath the window with a few odd pieces on it to hint that there were things inside the building. An HO scale oil drum and a few scraps of plastic did the trick.

Another oddity I had to disguise was the angled base where the kit stairs were supposed to be attached on one wall. First I cut off the two mounting pins from the back of the stairs and plugged the holes in the wall with them. Then I filed the area smooth. I made a phone box by cutting a piece of ¼" square Evergreen at a 45-degree angle, which I topped off with a small piece of .020 sheet that overhung all edges except the back. I bonded this at the bottom of the angled area. To give a purpose to the rest of the angled area, I added a conduit made from a small piece of .020 music wire that I bent to shape and chemically blackened. I then inserted the ends into holes I drilled in the wall. That completed the yard office, a rather simple undertaking.

THE ELEVATED GRADE CROSSING SHANTY

The yard office was so simple, yet this structure is just the opposite. The results, though, are well worth the effort. Of the four upper walls left, the one with the door and the opposite one are designed to be fastened to the backs of the other two walls. These were the walls that I narrowed while leaving the other two alone.

I cut the wall with the door right down the middle. This is a vertical cut as shown in fig. 5-1. As fig. 5-1 shows, I cut one window off of the opposite wall. It is the left window that I cut off. I made a vertical cut right in the middle of the space between this window and the three to the right. Because the plastic is brittle I used a saw and did not try to cut it with a knife.

SOME OPTIONS

I used the door half for my shanty, but you could use the clapboard half; first, you should decide whether you want to enter by stairs or a ladder. Many of these elevated shanties had a trapdoor in the floor, accessed by a ladder. If you are cramped for space, a ladder is the better choice, since the stairs require extra space. In either case, you would bond the single window to whichever half wall you choose.

Next, I bonded all four walls together. I would have liked to remove one window from the remaining two walls, making a square building, but I didn't because the shingle pattern on the sides would not match up correctly.

A NEW FLOOR AND ROOF

For the floor and the roof, I used Evergreen .040 V-groove siding with .100 spacing. Then I cut the floor to match the dimensions of the bottom of the walls. If you look closely at fig. 5-3, you may be able to see where I goofed when I first added a small platform by the door and then decided to remove it. I should have removed it all, but I left vestiges that plagued me when I added the stairs later. (Here's a case of where you should do as I say not as I did.)

I added seven .040 x .100 joists evenly spaced across the narrow dimension of the floor bottom. I also added strips of .060 square around the floor perimeter that would butt against the inside of the four walls. I adjusted these to be a force-fit and made sure none would interfere with any of the locating tabs that secured the walls together.

THE PEAKS

I then cut new peaks to go atop the narrow walls; for this I used Evergreen .040 clapboard with .080 spacing, matching the kit clapboards almost exactly. Figure 5-2 shows the shape I used. I bonded these in place using .030-thick fillers on the back of the clapboard to bring it out flush to the outer surface of the wall tops. Then I bonded these fillers to a scrap of styrene that stretched from the fillers to the back of the main walls.

THE ROOFS

Once the peaks were bonded, I measured the peaked sides and cut two roofs from the same stock as the floor. I used the grooves on the underside and measured to make roof panels two "boards" longer than the peaked sides. I then measured the other dimension and added ½" to it to provide a ¼" overhang at each end. Next, I removed .040 (the thickness of the V-groove material) from the top of one roof panel. This allowed me to bond the two panels together and butt the shorter one against the longer one at the top of the peak and have both panels the same

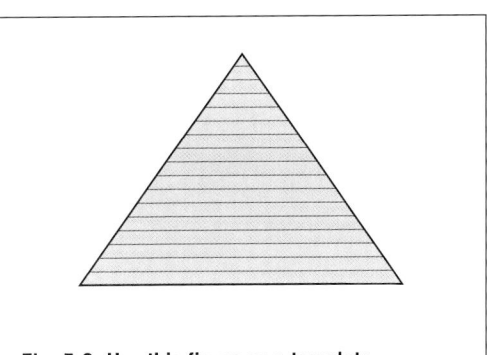

Fig. 5-2. Use this figure as a template for cutting the two peaked ends.

height. I added two strips of .020 x .188 strip at the peak for a cap. I did the same thing to these strips, removing .020 from one (the thickness), and bonded these to the peak. I overlapped these in the opposite direction of the main panels to provide a stronger joint.

I actually cut four identical peaks and used two of them, which I shortened at the bottom, around which I assembled my roof panels. I did this so I had a completed roof that I could bond to the peaks after I had painted the walls and put in the glass. I then added the smokestack, which is a Grandt Line product, to the roof.

THE SUPPORTS

Before installing the Plastruct ⅜" open web truss beams to support the shanty, I had to determine the building's height. The first step in that process was to assemble the Plastruct stairs and railings. The stairs seemed to be at a 45-degree angle, so I had two choices: I could use the railings with a vertical at the top and bottom, using four verticals total, or I could use three verticals, making the shanty ¾" lower. I felt this was too low. Having settled on a height for the stairs, I made a base from .080 sheet that measured 6" long x 1⅝" wide. I added .100 strips around the bottom perimeter and across at two places in between. This increased the height to a little more than ⅛".

I made my support beams 3⅜" long and bonded these to the floor and the first joist from the ends. I added a few more .040 x .100 braces around the tops of the beams because there is very little of the beam itself to bond to the floor. I used some bracing to wedge the beam against the outside joist and the first joist.

I added two angle braces made from Evergreen .030 x .125 styrene strip to the side of each support beam. They are 1" long and represent metal braces. I filed the ends at an angle that matched the surface to which each end was to be bonded. I cut small pieces of the same strip to go at each point where the braces joined the beam or the underside of the floor. These were less than ⅛" long. When placed at the end of the braces, they made the braces look as if they had an angle bent at the ends where bolts would secure them to the beam sides and floor bottom. I filed the ends of these small pieces at an angle prior to cutting them from the piece of strip.

Next, I bonded the beam bottoms to the base, using .040 square strip against the beams and the base in as many places as I could. I then added a ⅛"-thick pad on the top of the floor in the center and near the beam opposite the stairs. I drilled a hole in this and tapped it with a 4-40 tap. I added a scrap of .080 pad on the underside of the base opposite the hole in the floor. I drilled and tapped this also. Then I threaded a piece of 4-40 rod up from the bottom of the base and through both tapped holes. (This rod represents the connection from the controls to the gate-lifting mechanism.) I cut off the portion that protruded through the floor and pad inside the building. You would be surprised at how much strength this metal rod provides in securing the building to the base. The building is still precarious, but not as much.

I then added the stairs. As an added precaution, I drilled two holes in the bottom step and the second step up that also went through the base. These holes would accept small steel pins force-fit into them. Besides the solvent I inserted four pins to secure the lower end of the stairs to the base. I added some extra braces at the side of the stairs to help secure them to the building in front of the door.

As an alternative to the steel lattice beam supports, many of these elevated shanties had wooden post supports, and you might want to substitute these. They are easier to bond because they have a bigger bonding area than the ends of the beams provided.

DETAILS AND PAINTING

I felt the beam supports were still a bit wobbly, so I made a small coal box from the V-grooved material to help secure one support beam to the base. Mine is ¹⁵⁄₁₆" wide by ⅝" deep and 6½ boards high at the back against the beam and 5 boards at the front. The top overhangs three sides and I used some Grandt Line hinges on the lid. I painted the back of the coal box before I placed it against the beam, and before bonding the two together, I painted the beams Floquil grimy black. I scraped the paint off the back of the beam before bonding the coal box to them.

I painted the building to match the Rico

Fig. 5-3. The small yard office next to the tower provides shelter plus tool and equipment storage for maintenance crews.

stations. This meant mixing three parts Floquil Armour yellow, one part antique white, a few drops of roof brown, and a few drops of Milwaukee Road brown. The underside of the roof is also painted the yellow. I painted the door roof brown, and I painted the roof, the stack, and the support beams grimy black. Last, I gave everything a spray of Testor's Dullcote.

GLASS AND SHADES

The glass is a bit tricky, since the double-hung windows require a top piece and a separate bottom piece. I used a long strip to cover all window tops and one to cover all window bottoms. I cut them either three or four windows wide, depending on which wall they reside. I used single panes on the lone window by the door. These are bonded to the back of the windows.

I cut the shades from buff-colored typing paper and bonded them to the back of the window "glass," as I had done on the three Rico Stations. Now I could bond the roof permanently to the peaks. As with the Rico stations, I did no weathering. (My railroad keeps their buildings in tiptop repair, as I hope yours does!)

CONCLUSION

There are a lot of window openings to see into so I made an attempt at detailing the interior, but unless your building is right up front, you'll find that it can't be seen. All I added inside was a pot-bellied stove made from two HO scale wooden barrels. I cut one in half and added one half to the top of the full barrel; then I added a square .030 top and a .080 base with the sides flared at an angle, making the bottom wider. The legs are .060 square strips beneath the angled base. The stovepipe is part of a sprue. I painted everything black.

So there you have it, a very simple building and a more complex one. Both fill a need and neither looks much like the thousands of interlocking towers that everybody else has.

The wooden loading dock on the extension is accessible to trucks on all three sides. The new concrete truck dock is in the middle of the lengthened main wall. This could just as easily be the trackside, if you wish.

These are the two sets used to make Bigg Industries.

6 Bigg Industries

Calling this factory building Bigg is a stretch of the imagination, because it is really not all that big, but I did stretch out the length of the original kit, so it is actually Bigger. Fortunately, the Lionel factory kit I used as a basis is semi-modular and provides two extra wall segments with large door openings. These extras are intended to be used as alternates to two windowed sections. To a kit-basher, finding extra parts in a kit is like finding gold. I used these extras to make the building bigger than the four-segment length shown on the box photo.

ROBBING PETER TO PAY PAUL

To start, I assembled all the side walls (including the two "golden" extras) according to the diagrams in the instructions. I located the two extra door sections right in the middle of each side wall. I filed the mating edges of the two peaked walls (parts no. 20 and no. 22) and used a brace or two across the joint before bonding them together.

To stretch the building even more, I took the three parts for the small side annex (no. 20, no. 21, and no. 22) and made an office entrance on one end. Where did I get the extra wall with the large window to make the second office side wall? I robbed it from the peaked end wall. I used the third annex wall (no. 21) as a template centered over the window area of the end wall (no. 6) with the bottom of wall no. 21 flush against the protrusion at the base of wall no. 6. Then I traced the outline of wall no. 21 onto the end wall, using a knife to scribe around the template wall. I continued to scribe until I cut through a portion of wall no. 6. Then I inserted a saw blade and finished the cut to the ends.

I have a favorite tool for this, an X-acto no. 13 saw blade inserted in a no. 1 handle. Make certain the teeth cut on the pulling stroke, because the blade will bend if you cut on the pushing stroke. Do this with all four cuts and then remove the newly created wall.

Next I filed all edges smooth. Then I filed and scraped a 45-degree angle on one end to match the 45-degree edge on the peaked wall. Bond these walls together (no. 21, no. 22, and no. 20 plus the new one) to form the new extension. Center this new extension on the opposite end wall, no. 33, and bond it in place. This comes out roughly in the centers of the pilasters. Use 3/16" square braces at these joints.

I saved the brown door and window for a future project. As I make a building, I accumulate extra parts, sort of a scrap box from which to draw. This way Peter gets paid back (eventually).

FILLING THE GAP

Removing the window area from wall no. 6 left a big, drafty hole in the end wall that had to be filled. The Lionel Freight Platform kit came to the rescue. I assembled this kit according to the instructions. Even though this is a snap-fit building, I glued it together with the exception of the roof sections and windows. The roofs will be glued on after the glass is inserted.

To get the platform to fit flat against the main end wall, I had to cut a notch into one corner to clear the pilaster. I placed the freight platform against the end wall to see where the notch was needed. I also filed off the edge of the platform that butts against the main wall. I filed it flush with the actual wall. Next, I drilled four holes through both walls and tapped for 6-32 screws. This held the two buildings together as I flowed on some cement to bond them solidly.

I had to shorten the freight platform roof overhang where it butts against the brick wall. I cut off the overhang, leaving the main roof sections a little long, and then filed the edges until they fit against the brick wall. One corner of the roof ran afoul of the pilaster, so I notched it where necessary.

THE OTHER ROOFS

When I extended the length of the main brick building by one extra wall segment, the kit roof was too short to fit. I became "Peter" once more and used the leftover roof parts from a project that used most of International Hobby Corp.'s two-stall engine house kit. Lacking this, a plain styrene roof could be made. I cut these apart where needed to span the new length and bonded them to the four beams, parts no. 9. There is enough of this roof to use on the office extension, too. I shortened the width and notched the rear corners to fit around the two brick pilasters. I bonded the roofs in place.

PAINTING WINDOWS AND DOORS

Next I taped the brown side doors, the upper end door, and the doors and windows of the freight extension to a piece of cardboard, and spray-painted them with a green that matched the molded window and door color pretty closely. I used a common hardware store spray enamel. When the paint dried, I bonded the pieces in place, scraping off the paint from the bonding surfaces to get a good bond. I

Fig. 6-1. This long, narrow industry building is not wide, but is rather long, with the brick addition on the front and a wooden extension at the rear.

61

Fig. 6-2. The kit side annex and the kit's wooden trackside loading dock is in the lengthened middle of the main building, making the additional office.

glued the other doors and windows in place on the brick building.

THE DETAILING CREW ARRIVES

Next, I built the kit loading platform and made a new concrete platform from .040 sheet styrene. It is a box with braces in the corner joints. I notched the back of the side pieces where they have to clear the base of the building and where they go around the pilaster. Then I bonded the platform to the walls. I made the stairs by stacking ten 3/4"-long 3/16"-square strips. File the edges of the steps smooth, after the solvent has hardened, and bond the steps to a base of .060 sheet. Bond this unit to the end of the platform and the wall.

I added a few sprue pieces to the roof as vent pipes, and I assembled and added the square kit vents to the top of the roof. (The larger tall stack is again courtesy of the International Hobby Corp. kit.) I detailed the platforms with a few barrels.

SUMMON THE PAINTERS AGAIN

I became the paint crew once again and painted the main platform and the freight extension platform Floquil primer gray. I then bonded the kit platform under the other center doorway and sprayed everything with Testor's Dullcote.

NO-NO WEATHERING

After this dried I did something you are never supposed to do: go over a lacquer paint (the Dullcote) with anything made with alcohol. The alcohol turns the lacquer white—a big no-no. But this is not a goof; instead, if done in a controlled way, it is a way to achieve a weathered look. Here's how I accomplished it

I mixed a little India ink with alcohol in a spray bottle and took the model outdoors and sprayed over everything. I let it dry, with good results on the walls but a blotchy effect on the flat roofs. To remedy this, I took some plain alcohol and added a little bit of the mix to it, making a very, very weak gray. Then I used a large brush and wiped off most of the weathering mix. It had become especially black on the white plastic loading dock, and I just wanted to tone that down a little to look like concrete. This cleansing did the trick. I frequently wiped the brush clean on a paper towel. The brush was easier to control than the helter-skelter spray.

I used another way to tone down and even up the gray: I re-sprayed with Dullcote, bringing the color back toward what I started with. Then I brushed on the ink-and-alcohol mix, rather than spraying it on.

I was able to use a technique that is forbidden and turn it around into a plus. If you are timid, just mix the ink in plain water with a little dish detergent and then spray that on, or use a water-based black paint wash.

This no-no method produces an amazing change each time I use it. The mortar turns black, the bricks turn pink, the platforms get darker, and the black roof turns gray as it dries right before your eyes.

THE GLAZIERS TAKE OVER

Last, I added glass to all windows and doors. The Lionel factory kit includes molded glass pieces, but the freight platform building does not. I cut and fit glass out of a sheet of .010 clear styrene and bonded the glass in all windows. Once the glass was in place on the freight platform, I bonded the roof sections on permanently.

CONCLUSION

By utilizing all of the kit components and adding an annex, I stretched the original Lionel Factory building into a long, lean industry structure. However, it's not so lean that I can't have plenty of freight cars and trucks coming and going in a Bigg way.

This building is a compact petroleum industry with separate components that can be arranged in many ways. The truck loading area is clearly visible.

The two Lionel kits used to make Term Oil

7 Term Oil Company

As you pass through any small town, you'll probably find an industry like this nestled against the railroad tracks. It is a typical small bulk oil-distributing depot that periodically receives tank cars of fuel or heating oil and occasionally a boxcar of grease and lube oil in cans or barrels. These substances are stored in the tanks and the small warehouse to be distributed to customers by truck. Term Oil Company is the smallest version possible and can be squeezed into a very small space on your layout. The three elements of this project can be arranged in many different ways to fit your space.

"TANKS FOR HO SCALE"

Every so often I use things designed for other scales, and the two Rix Products tanks in this project are a good example. In HO scale they are 60 feet tall and 24 feet in diameter. In O scale they are 34 feet tall by 13½ feet in diameter. I assembled them following the directions, since the segments have to be assembled in order with the ones with the most rivets at the bottom and those with the least at the top.

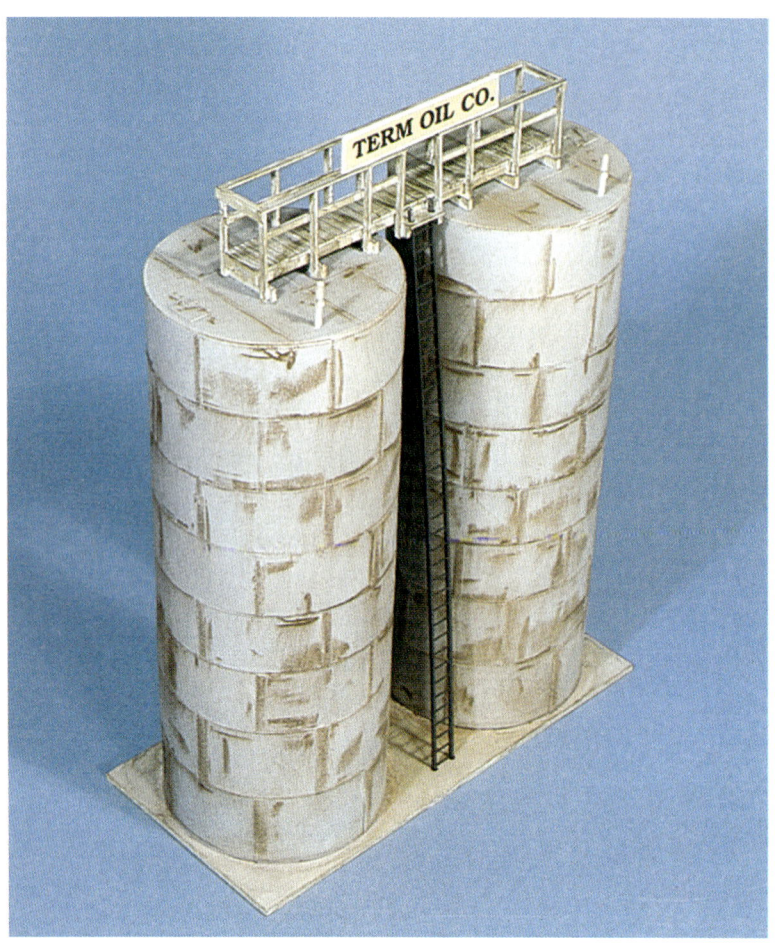

Fig. 7-1. A close-up of the wooden platform added to the tops of the tanks.

on top is a typical wooden affair. Some oil facilities have metal platforms and railings and you might want to try your hand at that. Plastruct has many railings that might work also.

Figure 7-2 shows how I made mine. The pieces may be a little oversized, but this platform adds considerable strength needed to hold the two tanks together. I even used three pins on each side of the assembly that went down through the platform and into the top of each tank to keep everything in line while the solvent set up. I inserted the pins in force-fit holes drilled for that purpose. The ladder is by Plastruct. Some old sprue parts bonded in holes in the tank top represent the tank vents.

THE PUMP HOUSE

I used a Lionel Barrel Shed to represent the pump house. I had used part of the platform and the legs on another project. All I had to do was fill in a gap in the base from which I had removed the platform part. I used a part of the kit handrail to fill the gap.

THE EVERYTHING-ELSE BUILDING

The wooden building that serves as a warehouse, office, and loading area for the delivery tank trucks is made from a Lionel Freight Platform kit. I did not modify this much at all, but I did shorten the front

The tanks are mounted on a base cut from .060 sheet to represent a concrete pad or foundation. I added some .060 strip around the edges and across the center to make the pad a little higher. The platform

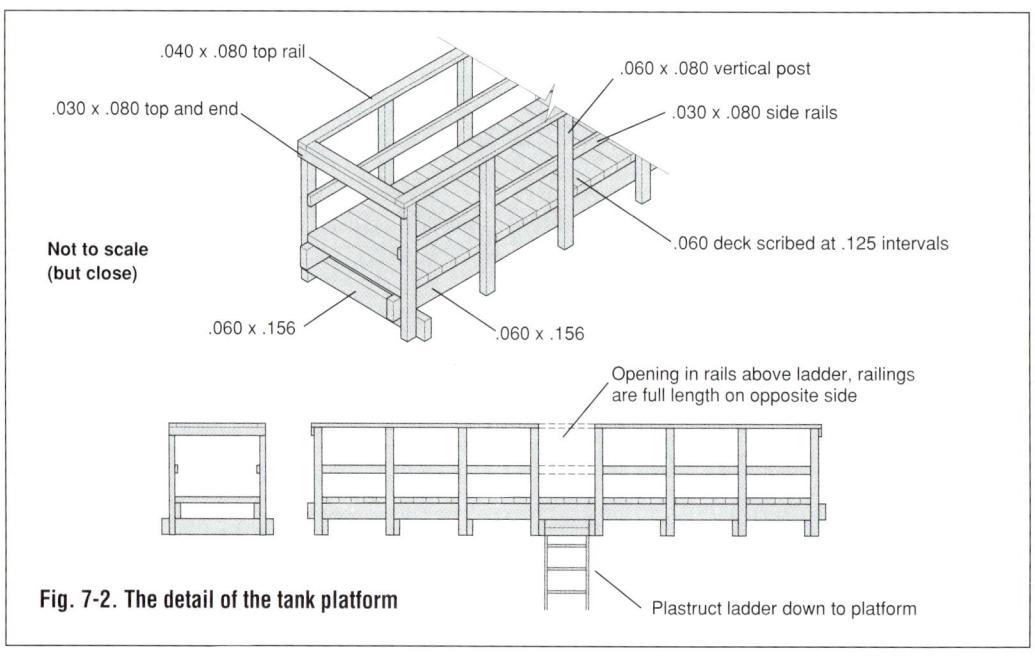

Fig. 7-2. The detail of the tank platform

Fig. 7-3. The opposite side of both wooden buildings. The Grandt Line door replaces the kit door, which was moved to the rear, or track side.

platform by cutting it off right between the first row of nails in from the front edge. I cut off the front post of each side leg assembly. Next, I added all of the leg assemblies in the appropriate grooves molded into the underside of the base. Then I cut off the end posts of the front end leg assembly but left the braces full length, sawing these off from the side. (They are needed later to bond to the two side end support posts.) I added this under the front edge of the platform.

I sawed vertical board separations in the end of the platform that I had cut off. It adds a lot of realism for a little effort.

I used a part of the platform I had cut off to make the angled ramp at the side of the platform. I cut a 2¼" length, with the edges filed at an angle to fit against the main platform and at the bottom, to rest on the ground. I added a piece of .125 square to represent a beam on the side that was cut from the original platform.

I also used small segments of the remaining platform to make a raised platform on top of the main one so workers could reach the truck loading pipes. I cut the four support legs and the three steps from the unused roof supporting posts.

THE WALLS

I assembled the walls and bonded them together, even though this is intended as a "snap together" building. I then added the front doors and the window on the side wall. I tossed the window from the back wall into my scrap box and used a Grandt Line baggage door to replace the kit side door. It had to be cut down in height to match the kit door. I cut a little from the bottom and more from the top. I had to make the top thinner to fit under the top door track using a straightedge to guide a knife with a chisel blade to thin the top portion that fits up under the door track. When you do this, pull the blade along the straightedge many times holding the blade 90 degrees to the door. Use slight pressure rather than trying to do it all in a few passes. This gives you much more control and limits slipping. Once the door fit, I glued on the door track. The new door will slide in the track just like the kit door if you want it to, but I bonded mine in place.

The back door uses the original kit door and it covers the window opening. I found a scrap of gray plastic that I used for a track above this door. I could have used a strip of .100 square. There is no smooth area on the wall for this door track, so I used pins at each end and in the middle to hold it on to the wall; otherwise, it would only bond to the tops of the battens on the wall. I did use solvent on the battens, and I also used .100 square strips to bond the door to the side of the window opening that this door covers. Last, I bonded the door to the batten tops with solvent.

I added this door so boxcars could unload here. If you don't need this feature, just assemble the building as intended. This building is actually a little small to have a full boxcar unload here, since it would fill up the entire warehouse with its contents, but I purposely overlooked that fact. (If you only use 40-foot boxcars to deliver the goods, it won't look so bad.)

A STEP UP

I could have used the kit stairs, but I wanted to add an extra touch of detail, so I used parts from a Grandt Line stair kit to make new ones that are a step up in quality. They are a little hard to hold together while assembling them, but the effort is worth it. Because the stairs are rather fragile, and stick out just begging to be broken off, I added a concrete foundation that supported them. I also added to this foundation some Walthers HO pipes from their pipe kit. The pipes run into the side or under the building and help justify the foundation's existence.

LESS ROOF

Since the platform was now shorter, the roof had to be shortened, too. I cut off the first section, keeping a raised portion at my new edge so it matched the rear edge. I sawed off the triangular overhang roof piece so the bottom edge was even and then made two triangular braces on .060 sheet stock that matched this kit part. I bonded the roof to these three triangles using scraps of .100 square strip between the roof and the triangles as braces. The two new triangles are hidden inside the building.

EVERYTHING HANGS TOGETHER WITH PAINT

A common color scheme makes all the elements look as if they belong together. In this project, the barrel shed is cream with a black door and windows, and I wanted this to match the larger building. I masked off the door and the windows with masking tape and spray-painted these with a hardware store flat gray primer. When this dried, I removed the tape and brush-painted the walls with Floquil Erie Lackawanna maroon. It closely matched the color of the main building, but not quite, so I painted the main building maroon also. The gray doesn't match exactly, and neither does the maroon, which covers cream on the barrel shed and maroon on the main building. Since the two buildings are a few scale feet apart, though, this difference is hardly noticeable.

I painted the platform with Floquil foundation and then brushed the India-ink-and-alcohol wash over it, making it look like real aged wood. Once this dried, I bonded the walls to the platform.

I painted the black tanks with a flat white spray and, you guessed it, they turned gray! I could have sprayed many more coats to make the tanks turn white,

Fig. 7-4. This side shows the pipes and the two Rix tanks.

Fig. 7-5. The back side of Term Oil shows the loading doors on the main building and the ramp leading up to the platform.

but I stopped when they looked right. Silver would also have been a good choice, but I didn't have any on hand. Tanks were commonly painted in either color to reflect the heat from the sun.

I drybrushed Floquil foundation on the wooden platform to make it look as if it was once painted white, but that some paint had begun to peel in places, exposing the bare wood. Then I gave this a wash of India ink and alcohol to match the platform look.

I used brown pastel chalk sticks to add rust to the tanks. I concentrated it mostly on the joints, seams, and rivets where rust would naturally form. To fix the chalk, I sprayed the tanks with Testor's Dullcote.

LET'S CHEAT

The most difficult detail to add is the pipes that load the oil delivery trucks. Some oil facilities have a separate loading platform, which is sometimes roofed, sometimes exposed. In either case they are a maze of pipes, pumps, and supports that befuddled me, so I cheated and decided to just hint at them. I added a bare minimum sticking out from under the platform roof. These pipes were also made from the Walthers HO pipe kit.

Walthers has an oil depot kit available, and you can use that or part of it and perhaps combine it with my version. Plastruct also has a few tank kits available and you could use the painting and weathering techniques I have shown you on any of these. However, Term Oil is a unique building, very different from the Walthers bulk oil depots.

CONCLUSION

With all the main parts done, it's time to do any extra weathering. I sprayed both building roofs with Dullcote. Then I brushed on the ink and alcohol wash, which lightened them as it dried. Last I added the window glass and some paper shades and fastened the roofs in place.

The earth surrounding this complex should have an oily look since there are many opportunities for spillage. In addition, scatter a few bright red oil drums around the platform, add a few workers and signs, and the Term Oil depot is ready for the local freight to spot a tank car at the siding and begin serving its customers.

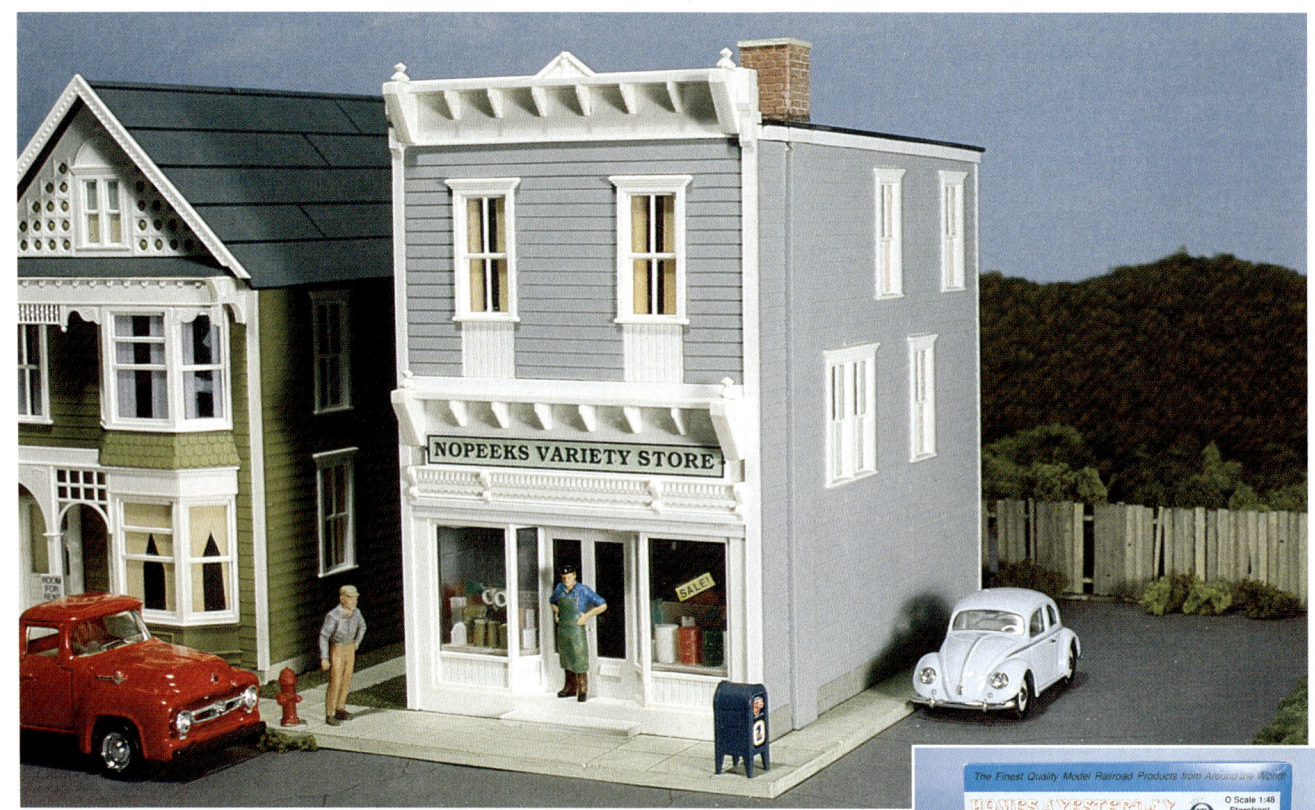

The Nopeeks store is a typical wooden building with fancy trim to enhance the facade. Stores like this could be found in any village or small city.

The far right kit is the one used for Nopeeks.

8 Nopeeks Variety Store

One of my definitions of kitmingling was to alter the look of a kit. Nopeeks is a good example because it started out as one of five storefront kits from International Hobby Corp. I call these kits pre-kitmingled, since they use parts from IHC's series of five "Painted Lady" Gingerbread San Francisco row houses. The storefront wall pieces are the only ones different from the "Painted Lady" houses. The only thing wrong with these is the way the windows are laid out.

THE BIG GOOF

The front walls in the storefront kits are two-story affairs, and the sides and back are three. I attempted to correct this design goof in my renovation of Nopeeks.

If you decide to make any modifications, such as those I will describe, choose either the South Street Smoke Shop or O'Weeds Greenery because the trim elements are molded in white styrene and you can easily match this to the white Evergreen styrene used in the alterations. This means no painting will be required.

THE BIG FIX

I chose O'Weeds Greenery to renovate into a more typical storefront. My first aim was to make the front look as if it could have three stories, all at normal height, thus matching the other three walls. I also wanted to make a major change by having a flat roof instead of a peaked one. In the process I was also able to eliminate the ugly three-window bay. Mr. Nopeeks wanted to occupy this building as soon as I finished, so I grabbed my knife and saw and plunged in.

DE-PEAKING

Note that I'll refer to the kit part numbers from time to time to aid in the identification of items.

I first assembled the upper window insert, part no. 51, and the storefront, part no. 52, into the wall frame, part no. 50. At this point I cut off the peaked portion of the front wall and the rear wall. This changed the look dramatically, which was one of my goals.

A LOSS AND A GAIN

Having tossed out the ugly bay, I had to find a way to fill the opening in the front wall occupied by the bay. To do this I had to find at least two extra windows. If I shortened the side walls and removed one window opening, I would gain one window. The walls were very long anyway, so I cut 9½ scale feet from the rear of wall part no. 11. (Make sure this vertical cut is along the inside [left] of the second-floor window on the right side of this wall.) Then cut off an equal amount from the windowless end of the opposite wall, no. 10.

The store kit instructions called for eight windows. The windows included are for a Painted Lady house for which nine windows are needed, so I took the extra one, plus the one I just gained, to help fill the opening. I could then assemble all the walls following the kit instructions.

FILLING THE VOID

To fill the bay opening, I placed the two windows I just gained in the upper right and upper left corners of the opening and bonded them in place. Then I measured the distance between them and cut a piece of that width from one of the wall pieces I had removed. I cut this to the height of the opening. I made sure to allow for some extra width so the new wall piece would slip under the lip on the sides of the windows. I filed the wall carefully to get a snug fit. Then I bonded this center piece in place with scrap styrene bracing across the joint on the inside.

I originally thought of using a few small pieces of clapboard cut from the leftover wall siding under the two windows, but it was easier to use two rectangles cut from scribed sheet to fill these spaces.

WINDOW FLIPPING

I next turned to the actual storefront. Here I flipped both larger windows and the smaller indented ones upside-down (part nos. 54, 55, 56, and 57). This meant the left one went where the right one was supposed to go, and so on. Only the door, part no. 53, remained in its original configuration. I bonded the upside-down windows and the door in place. (I scribed a line down the center of the door to split it into two halves, something the manufacturer forgot to do.) Next I added small pieces of scribed sheet styrene behind the open areas (originally windows atop the main windows) that were now at the bottom.

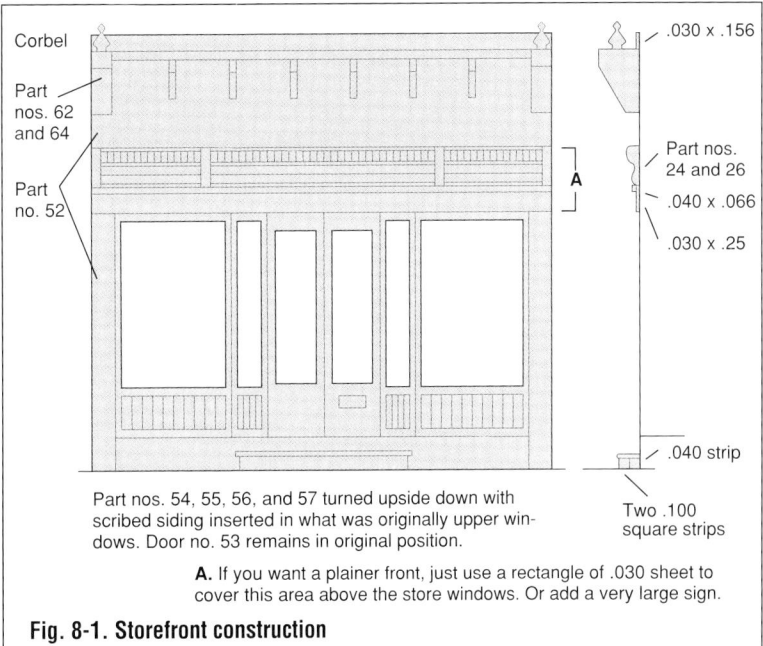

Part nos. 54, 55, 56, and 57 turned upside down with scribed siding inserted in what was originally upper windows. Door no. 53 remains in original position.

A. If you want a plainer front, just use a rectangle of .030 sheet to cover this area above the store windows. Or add a very large sign.

Fig. 8-1. Storefront construction

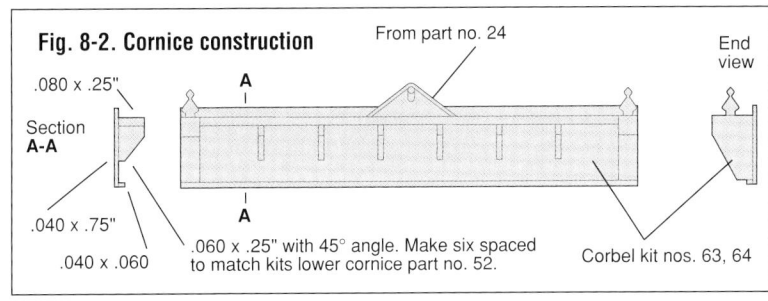

Fig. 8-2. Cornice construction

Fig. 8-3. The only thing added to the rear is a small roof over the back door. The roof detail can also be seen.

USING UP THE EXTRAS

There are many extra parts on the white sprue with the windows that were for use on the Painted Lady houses. Using part nos. 24 and 26, two of the fancy trim pieces from this sprue, I made a new trim that went across the top of the window area. I sawed off the things that look like ladders and the peaked thing on part no. 24. (Save that peaked part!) I filed all edges flat. I used the longest part on the right and a short segment from the part with the peak removed on the left side. I placed these together and determined where the longest one had to be cut to meet the shortest one and still span the window area fully. I cut here, and bonded this above the store window opening. I also added a .030 x .156 strip across at the top to help hide the joint between the cornice and the gray window insert above it. I then used an .030 x 250 piece at the bottom across the tops of the large storefront windows. I added a strip of .040 x .060 across the top of this strip. (See fig. 8-1 and the photos.)

FANCY TIMES TWO

Quite often you will find that an architectural detail is repeated on a structure, and that's the case here. The kit provided four fancy corbels—part nos. 63 and 64—and this kit called for them to be placed by the cornice over the store windows and again near the peaks. I carried out that theme a little further when making the cornice atop the front wall. It mimics the trim above the storefront.

I took a piece of .040 sheet, cut it to match the width of the front wall, part no. 51, and made it ¾" high. I added a strip of .040 x .060 across the bottom. Then I placed the two corbels at the extreme ends. Next I cut a piece of .080 x .250 strip to go between the corbels. Then I took a piece of .060 x .250 strip and cut segments at 45 degrees about 5/16" long. I cut these on my NorthWest Short Line chopper to ensure exact matches. Even taking these precautions, I cut 12 in order to get 6 that were perfectly matched. (See fig. 8-2 and the photos.)

I added these six under the .080 horizontal piece spaced to match the lower example. Next I added the triangular trim piece I had removed earlier (and saved) and centered it at the top. Now I had my repeated cornice. I did not make the seven small details between the verticals because they were a complex diamond shape that I could never duplicate. They are very small and I felt they would not be noticed if they weren't there. (You probably would not have known it if I hadn't just told you!)

GETTING IT ALL TOGETHER

Next I added the vertical kit trim, part no. 22, at the two back corners. Since I needed taller trim for the front because of the new taller cornice, I used .080 x .156 strip. I added a few more braces across the back of the cornice for good measure. The lower one was 1/8" square and the upper .060 sheet about 1/4" wide. Later I bonded two pieces of .080 x .156 trim at each side of the corbel. After they set up solid, I filed the edges flat where needed.

I added the back door and all the windows. I even snuck in one of the extra small windows, part no. 16, on side wall no. 10 by cutting an opening in the wall for it.

WE'RE GETTING TO THE TOP

I cut the flat roof from a piece of .080 sheet with at least a 3/16" overhang on all three sides. (Cut it a little wider and longer to allow making up any errors in squareness of the building. The front of the roof butts against the back of the cornice.) Next I added .080 x .156 trim boards under the roof on each side, except the front, that would allow the walls to fit snugly within the trim boards. To give the roof a slight pitch from front to back, I added a piece of .080 x .156 strip on the underside of the roof across the front, 1/4" back from the cornice. This raised the front by .156 since this cross-piece sits on top of the side walls.

I had to add a small triangular piece atop the slope of the chimney flue on the side of the building wall. I filed this from a piece of scrap wall until I got a reasonable fit, then bonded it on. I added a piece of scrap styrene to the roof trim board, presumably a jog in the trim to fit around the chimney flue. Then I added to the roof a vent pipe made from a piece of scrap sprue and a hatch from two rectangles of .080 sheet. I put the smaller rectangle on the bottom and centered the larger one on top of it.

Next I assembled the kit chimney, part nos. 3, 4, 5, and 6, and sawed the bottom to match the roof pitch. I added a cap made of four pieces of .080 x .156 strip since I lost the kit cap. I had to go back and add two small pieces of .080 x .156 inside the two roof trim strips to fill a gap behind the cornice.

The last detail I added was a small roof over the back door. In keeping with the no-peak theme, I made a slightly sloped roof from .060 sheet. It is as wide as the double window and an inch deep. I glued .080 x .060 strip trim pieces around all sides. I placed these on the bottom of the roof 1/16" back from three sides and flush with the back. Once this set up, I filed the back so it had an angle, giving the roof a slight slope toward the outer edge. Next I added two braces of .060 x .080 strip. I placed these so they angled from the outer edge of the roof toward the rear wall. I placed small scraps of the same strip at the bottom of the braces against the wall.

BACK TO EARTH

Next, I turned to the base. I placed the shortened building on it to see what could be done to utilize it. One thing I found was that the store was originally supposed to sit into the base, not on top of it, so by removing sections of the base and gluing it back together I was able to place the building on top of a smaller base. If the building was set into the base, there was no need for a front step; with it on top, I had to add a front step. I made the step from two pieces of .100 square strip placed side by side, with a piece of .040 sheet on top. This would prevent Mr. Nopeeks from being sued if someone tripped over a too-tall step (see fig. 8-1).

I scribed in some new sidewalk squares by the back door and added a few cracks here and there. I painted the sidewalk Floquil antique white and the foundation blocks concrete.

Next I added the sign. Fortunately this hides the fancy relief trim that looks like a bunch of connected rectangles. I knew my sign would cover these and that's why there was no need to duplicate these when I made the top cornice.

CONCLUSION

With the building complete, I painted the roof black and sprayed everything with Dullcote. Then I added the window glass and some printed curtains supplied in the kit. I placed a few things in the showroom window awaiting the arrival of the new owner. Mr. Nopeeks' storefront is certainly quite different from those other four that IHC makes. In fact, he said it had "Nopeeks written all over it."

This is a typical small-town retail coal dealership. Behind the small office is the angled coal conveyor leading to the twin storage bins.

This photo shows one kit built the way it is supposed to be made.

9 Kold Coal Company

For years coal was the choice for home heating and most towns had a dealer that received coal via the railroad. These firms stored the coal in a large bin and then delivered it to the customer when needed. Most of these have been supplanted by oil depots serving the same purpose (see Chapter 7 on the Term Oil Company).

Since many model railroads are set in an era when steam engines still were huffing and puffing along the rails, I thought a retail coal dealer would fit into this era very comfortably. There is no typical one available, so I set out to make one that Mr. Jacob Kold might have had back in 1927.

THE DOUBLE BIN

I used two recognizable Bachmann Plasticville coaling stations to make the bin. First I sawed off the peaked portion of all of the side walls right at the place where they rise above the rest of the wall. Then I filed off the ends of the three horizontal beams at the A and C ends of the side walls, making this surface even. (These letters refer to the letters molded into the backs of the kit walls.) These ends

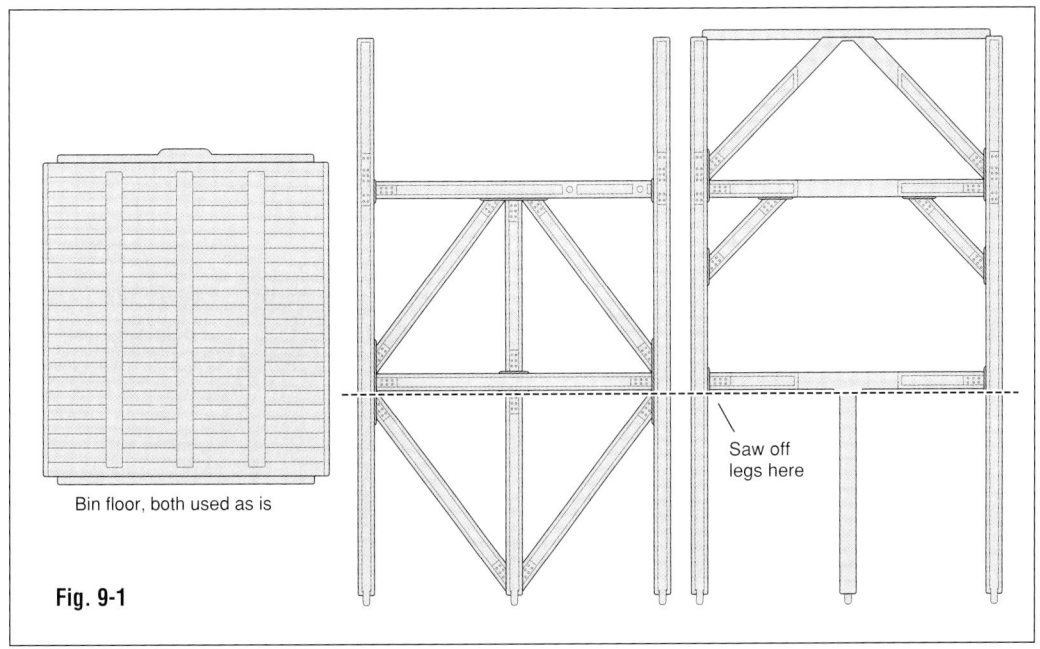

Fig. 9-1

Bin floor, both used as is

Saw off legs here

must butt together, so I filed them perfectly flat.

Next I sawed off the bottom section of the steel beam support legs below the first horizontal beam up from the bottom. This lowered the height of the bin.

BASIC BIN ASSEMBLY

Next I assembled one bin and its support legs but omitted rear wall H F. I made sure the rear support legs were placed as they should be, according to the assembly instructions, with the riveted plate areas of the beams toward the outside. I then filed off half of the little nub at the end of the large horizontal bottom beam on the second bin sides. This nub was supposed to fit into the opening in the rear of the steel beam, but since this second bin is attached to the side of the beam with the rivet plates sticking out, I had to file the nub off to clear the plate. Once I did this, I test-fitted the sides of the second bin, and, when satisfied they would fit, I bonded the three walls of the bin to the first bin. I used a few pieces of scrap styrene across the butt joint on the inside to strengthen it.

Then I added the other front steel support beam to the front of the second bin, riveted plate side out, and added the two bin floors. Since there is no rear wall, there is a gap at the top of the sloped bin floors. I filled the gap with a long rectangle of sheet styrene cut to fit so that if you

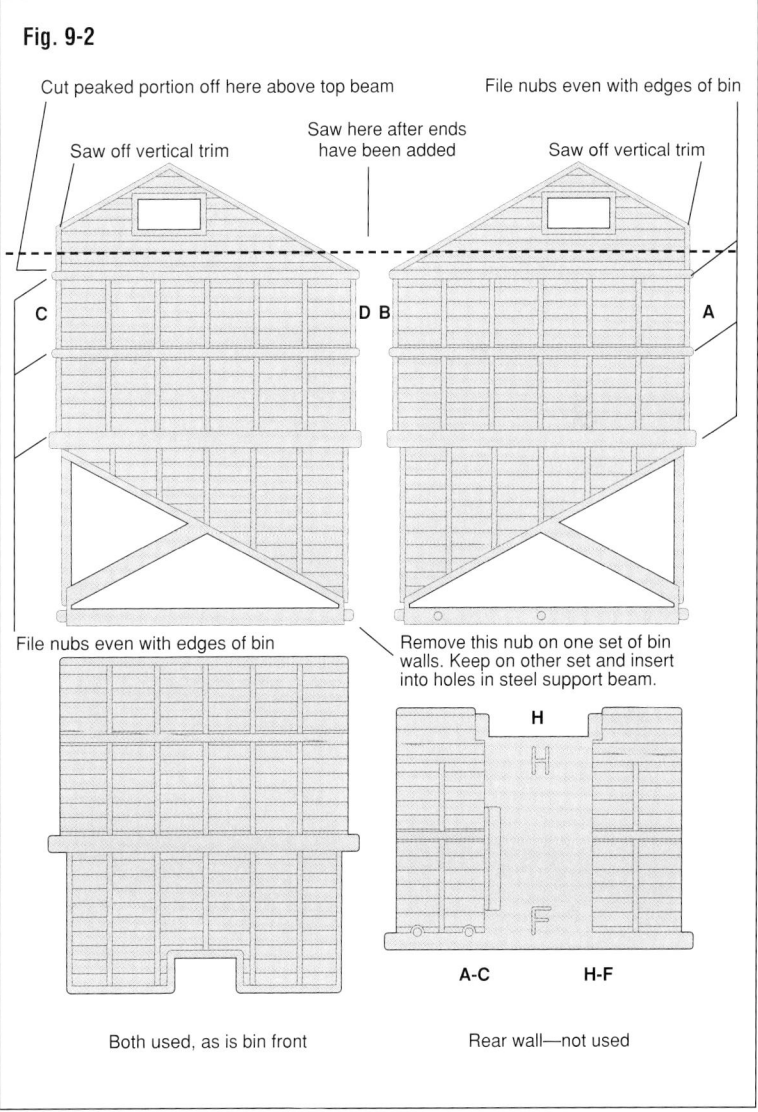

Fig. 9-2

Cut peaked portion off here above top beam
File nubs even with edges of bin
Saw off vertical trim
Saw here after ends have been added
Saw off vertical trim

C   D B   A

File nubs even with edges of bin
Remove this nub on one set of bin walls. Keep on other set and insert into holes in steel support beam.

A-C   H-F

Both used, as is bin front
Rear wall—not used

73

looked in an end window, you wouldn't see an opening there.

There are two holes on the side of two of the horizontal wooden beams. These are where the nubs of the railing are supposed to be inserted. Since I am not using this railing, I plugged these holes with a long sliver of styrene about 1" long that I cut from the unused kit rear wall. I cut it square and rounded the edges a bit and then, using lots of solvent, forced the end into a hole. I repeated this with a twisting motion a few times, each time adding more solvent that melted both the plug and the opening until I got a snug fit with no gaps. Then I cut off the end of the plug a bit long and used the rest to plug the second, third, and fourth holes the same way. I let this set up a long time and then filed the area flat so there was no sign of a hole when I was done. There are similar holes on the steel beam, but I left these alone.

THE NEW PEAKS

Now I returned to the four peaks I had cut off the sides earlier. First I sawed off the vertical trim on the ends of a left and a right peak. I sawed off a small triangular segment from the remaining left and right peaks (remember that there are two each since I am using two kits) that enabled me to match the opposite side of the peak. I bonded these to the first set of peaks to make two complete triangular peaks without any flat end like the original peaks. I used small scraps of sheet styrene across the joint on the back. I let this joint set up overnight.

In the morning after this joint was totally solidified, I sawed off the bottom of the two newly made triangular peaks two boards up from the bottom. This shortens the width so the new peaks will fit above what was the two kit front walls with just a little overhang when centered above these walls.

THE NEW ROOF

Now that I had two triangular peaks, I could make a new roof to span the two bins. (The kit roofs are not large enough to be reused on the larger bins.) For my new roof I cut two pieces of .060 sheet styrene 9⅜" long by 3" wide. I filed the mating peak edges at an angle so they would meet with a minimal gap when joined together.

Then I added the two new peaks to the bottom of the new roof pieces. When working on your roof, be sure that the peaks are equal distances in from both ends and will rest squarely upon the tops of the two front walls. Do this before the bond has set up fully and adjust the peaks in or out while the joint between the peaks and roof is still soft. I added .100 square strips inside at the joint of the peaks and the underside of the roof for additional strength. I also utilized the other two leftover peaks that the small segments were cut from, by bonding them to the underside of the roof equidistant from the end peaks. This strengthened the roof peak joint considerably. I did not bond the new roof to the end walls yet; I still had things to do that required access to the inside of the bins. I did add some diamond mesh fabric, called tulle, inside the two end windows. I also cut two small squares of brown scrap from one of the unused kit rear walls and added one at each side of the bins on top of the center steel beam supports. These now look like the ends of a center wooden beam, just like the two beams that rest on the tops of the other outer steel supports (see fig. 9-4).

THE CONVEYOR

Next I tackled the new conveyor. I first had to cut off the area at the top with the door opening, which I did, two boards below the bottom of the door. Then I took this conveyor and added a portion from the second conveyor on top. I cut the second piece 2½" long from the bottom above the chute door opening. I attached this to the top of the first full-height conveyor with appropriate scrap braces on the inside. I also cut a 2½"-segment from the conveyor back and bonded this to the back of the three-sided part, but staggered the joints for strengthening purposes. Here I put the small segment at the bottom and the full back at the top. Next I added the chute door at the bottom of the full-length segment. This door has random-length boards that I felt looked too haphazard, so I cut off the ends of the longest ones to even things out a bit.

After everything set up firmly, I measured the width of the conveyor. I then cut a notch out of the middle of one side of the roof to that width and in, to the edge of the side wall. The top of the conveyor sits in this notch. Next I placed the roof on top of the bins, not yet permanently fastened, and determined at what angle the bottom of the conveyor had to be cut to make it rest flat on the ground. I then cut off the bottom of the conveyor at this angle, leaving the chute door full height. I placed the conveyor back against the roof to find out what size triangle would be needed to extend the back of the conveyor into the roof side. I used a small piece of file card to cut and trim until it fit and then transferred this shape to .060 sheet styrene. I cut two sides to this shape. Figure 9-3 is a template that is a good beginning, but use this only as a guide to start your own template.

Next I bonded the two triangular pieces to the roof and then used these as a guide to cutting off the top of the conveyor so a flat roof could cover both areas. I cut the conveyor top at this angle. You might want to make the triangular template so there is more of a pitch to the roof, as mine wound up almost flat with just a slight pitch toward the main rooftop peak. Once I was satisfied everything was fitting properly, I cut a roof from .060 sheet to fit over the conveyor and the extension.

Before bonding the conveyor to the roof, I cut an opening in the outer wall at the top so I could insert a door. Since there is one door in each kit, I had two at my disposal and could have used one here. However, since the conveyor was now on an angle, rather that vertical, I felt a door with no window would be more appropriate, so I used a solid Grandt Line door and cut the opening to accommodate it. I used a small pin as a doorknob and force-fitted it in a hole that I had drilled in the door. I placed the knob down low so it can be reached easily from the ladder.

I used the kit's long, lower stairway to lead up to the door. I cut off the side railings and the top portion of the stairway even with the two side rail supports so the door could open out with no interference. I also cut off the lower stair sides below the first step. This allowed the stairway to rest flat on the clapboard conveyor side and while still sitting above the raised chute door. This gave me more bonding area with all the stairs resting on the clapboard tips. Last, I bonded the conveyor to the two triangular roof extensions with .125 braces in the interior corners and then fastened the roof on top.

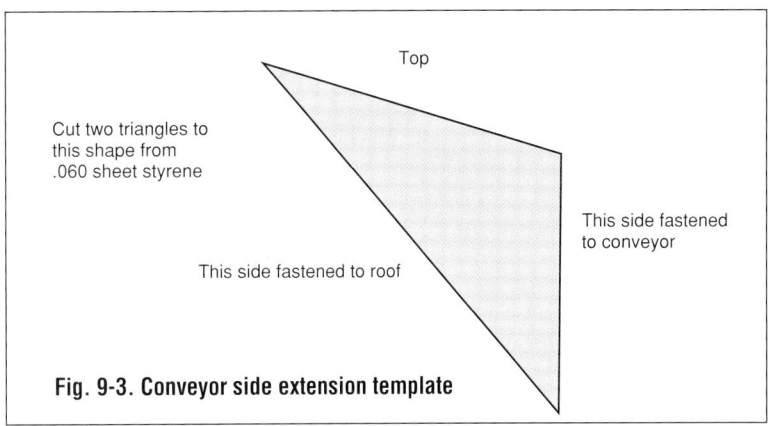

Fig. 9-3. Conveyor side extension template

THE HIDDEN SHED

Since I like to utilize every part of a kit if possible, I decided to make a small storage shed/scale house to go beneath the bins. I made this from the top part of the conveyor with the door opening. I cut a matching piece from the second conveyor and made the roof pitch match the other piece. Then I bonded these back to back and added a roof cut from one of the kit corrugated roofs on top.

I had the luxury of two unused rear bin walls, which allowed me to cut many brown pieces from them to be used where needed. I cut a piece of scrap brown plastic, equal to the height of the door, from the unused kit rear wall and added this to the left side of the door opening. I also added another small piece as a door sill, since the opening was originally designed to have a part of the platform project into the door opening. These scraps made the opening smaller so the door would fit snugly. I bonded the door permanently in place.

This shed helps hide the notches cast into the rear of the steel supports where the vertical conveyor was supposed to be inserted. I also added a half beam, with an E cast into the back, that I cut off the bottom of the one unused rear steel beam support leg piece. I added this to the center support under the new bins. I also added a piece of full beam right above this one to help support the center of the bin. After all, this set of supports carries the weight of both parts of the bins. I cut a small notch in one edge of the shed roof to clear the top vertical beam I had just added.

A SOLID CONCRETE BASE

I wanted to have a strong base to tie the conveyor and fragile legs together; I cut a

Fig. 9-4. This view shows the end of the wooden beam that is at the top of the center steel support.

T-shaped piece from a sheet of .060 styrene. One sheet was not wide enough to include the bottom end of the conveyor, so I cut three separate pieces and assembled them to make a base. To tie these pieces together and to add some thickness, I used .125 square strip around the perimeter, across the joints and across a few other places. I also added some rectangular .060 scraps across the joints on the underside. I did leave an opening in the base beneath the shed so I could add glass in the lone window after all weathering was done. I also added strips of .060 under all three support legs to raise them above the main base. I added the same under the conveyor bottom. At this point I bonded the base to the legs, making a very strong unit. I was worried about the conveyor being very vulnerable since it was sticking out there all by itself, so I bonded the shed to the base and steel support beams. I added .100 x .156 strip around the base at the bottom as a foundation for the shed.

WEIGH THAT COAL

Jacob Kold wanted to make sure he gave every customer the exact amount of coal for which they had paid, right down to the last lump. To assure this, I added a scale on top of the platform, under the bin opposite the shed. It is a piece of .030 sheet in which I scribed wooden planks. These planks were ¼" wide. The outside is surrounded by a concrete rim, also ¼" wide. All this is scribed on the sheet that is 3" wide by 4¼" deep. I scribed the main grooves deep and then added shallower wood grain on most boards. I painted the boards with Floquil foundation, and then, after this dried, I brushed on my ink-and-alcohol mix to settle in the scribed grooves and darken the wood. I bonded the scale to the base.

If your delivery truck is larger than mine, the scale will probably be too short. You could add some length to the base and make a longer scale or have a separate one at another location, possibly next to the office.

THE END ROOFS AND COAL CHUTES

I wanted to add small roofs over the coal chutes at each end, so I cut four triangles from the leftover part of one of the kit conveyor back pieces. I cut these six boards tall and angled the pitch to the other side. Then I cut two rectangles from .060 sheet 1⅝" deep by 4¼" wide for the roofs. I bonded the triangles to the front and against the inside of the steel beam supports. Then I added the roof on top of these and placed it against the underside of the large wood horizontal beam. I had to cut small notches in both ends to clear the steel vertical beam, I filed the top of the roof edge to give it some surface to attach itself to the underside of the wooden beam. I could have notched the roof edge so it would go around all five vertical beams and have more bonding surface, but I did not. I did use the four scrap triangular segments, which I got from cutting the four end roof braces, in the center as added support for the roof. I cut these down to four boards so they would not be readily seen. (I made sure I used only the four triangles with the clapboard right side up on the outside.)

The kit supplies two coal chutes. I decided to make mine smaller, so I used the kit footings to make narrower chutes. I cut off the ends of one footing, each piece being 2" long. Then I cut two ⅞" long segments from the kit chute. I added these to the top of the smaller chutes to help fill the opening in the front wall that was designed for the wider chute. The new chutes are bonded to the bin floor top. They protrude from the outer wall about 1½"—not a critical length (see fig. 9-2).

ON GOES THE ROOF

Once the chutes were bonded in place, I did not need to do any more work on the interior, so I could bond the roof to the end walls and the conveyor bottom to the base. I added scrap pieces of sheet styrene to the backs of the end peaks and flowed solvent on them heavily. I then placed the roof on, ran solvent at the joint of the wall tops and peak bottoms, and pressed the roof in place. I also flowed lots of solvent around the conveyor bottom to fasten it to the base. To be doubly safe, I drilled two holes into the bottom edge of the coal chute door of the conveyor into the base and force-fit steel pins into these holes. I used short ends of the pins, about ⅜" long. I did the same thing at the four corners of the roof. Here I drilled holes through the roof and into and through the top of the side walls. I drilled almost 90 degrees to the roof, which meant the hole was angled through the side wall. These six pins added much to the strength and tied everything together solidly.

ROLL ON THE ROOFING

To simulate asphalt roll roofing, I cut some reddish-brown construction paper into ¾" strips. I began at the bottom and placed these against the roof and then flowed solvent through them from the top surface of the paper. The paper soaked it up like a blotter, and the solvent softened the plastic roof enough to bond the paper in place. I overlapped each successive strip as I moved toward the top peak. When I ran out of a full strip, I butted a second one right next to it. I did both sides of the roof and then added a ridge piece that was about ½" wide. I folded this one down the center prior to adding it at the top. I also had to cut out one side to go around the conveyor roof extension. I added these strips to the conveyor rooftop. I went back to my template for the roof extension and used it to cut two side pieces from the construction paper. I bonded these to each side. I had to cut pieces ⅞" wide for the end chute roofs. With the overlap, there would be a small strip of paper roof at the top and very little of the plastic roof sur-

Fig. 9-5. From the back you can see the scale beneath one bin for weighing the truck empty. The truck is then weighed when full to determine how much coal is going to the customer.

face to which to bond the paper, so I used the wider strips to overcome this. When all of the paper roofing dried, I sliced off any excess that hung out over the edges with a sharp new knife blade.

WEATHERING AND DETAILS

With the bins completed, I sprayed everything with Dullcote. Then I sprayed on my alcohol-and-ink mix, which turned almost everything gray. I then sprayed on a second coat of Dullcote, which brought back most of the colors to brown, but darker, since the black ink remained. I gave it a second coat of my mix. The same thing happened, gray again. On went another coat of Dullcote spray, which got rid of the gray. The brown was darker yet. I was getting closer to where I wanted to be, so I gave it one more sequence and left it alone. As far as I was concerned, the third time was a charm! I used this technique of spraying on a final coat of Dullcote whenever the alcohol-and-ink mix made things overly gray.

I did have to go back and repaint the roof since I really did not have the red paper I wanted in the first place. Besides, the roof had begun to curl up at the edges and I had to glue them down with thinned Elmer's white glue. Then I could paint the roof with Floquil AT&SF mineral brown. I added a few black tar patches since this was an older building and would have

Fig. 9-6. This angle shows the small weigh shed beneath the bins and the roof over the truck-loading chutes.

presumably needed some repairs during its lifetime.

Now I added the glass in the lone window. I also added a waste barrel, some spilled coal, and debris scattered around the base. I made a ladder and placed it against the coal loading chute so the main stair was accessible. I placed this at the base of the conveyor.

JACOB NEEDED AN OFFICE

Mr. Kold needed a place to take care of the paperwork, so I made an office, a separate kitmingle ail by itself. I used two shanties, no. 901 and no. 903, made by AM Models. I made the larger one, no. 903, following the instructions. No. 901 is smaller and has two side walls identical to the three windowed walls of no. 903, plus two smaller end walls with peaks. One of these has a door, and the other is plain. I cut off the peaks on these, even with the top of the door frame. Then I cut the top of each of the larger walls at an angle. The lower part was even with the door top and the other end was $1/16$" from the top.

I added pins for doorknobs and a Grandt Line smokestack to the roof plus a sprue vent pipe. Naturally, Jacob Kold had a small coal stove inside to keep the office toasty in the winter.

I weathered the office using the same technique as on the main bin. Then I made a base from .080 sheet by tracing the outline and adding about $1/16$" all around and adding two doorsteps. Then I attached the glass and paper window shades and bonded the building to the base. You can use this little office as I show it here, or you could use it with another industry or as a railroad yard office.

CONCLUSION

You might consider Kold Coal to be a destination for your hopper cars. It is a kitmingle that has very recognizable beginnings, but certainly changes a lot in the transformation.

Fig. 9-7. The Kold Coal office is made by combining the two AM Models kits. This is the rear view.

APPENDIX A: SIGNS

TIPAKULL
Manufacturing Co.

NOPEEKS VARIETY STORE

KOLD
COAL

BURNS CLEAN

A
H
·
S
O
·
W
A
T

CHINESE
CUISINE

A
H
·
S
O
·
W
A
T

CHINESE
CUISINE

Billy's
Barber Shop
& Billiards

Billy's
Barber Shop
& Billiards

Dewey
Cheatem
& Howe
Attorneys
At Law

KOLD
COAL

BURNS CLEAN

ACME
REALTY

Dewey
Cheatem
& Howe
Attorneys
At Law

LUCKY
MALONEY'S
IRISH PUB

FLEECE
and
STEEL
LOANS

KOLD
COAL

BURNS CLEAN

LUCKY
MALONEY'S
IRISH PUB

FLEECE
and
STEEL
LOANS

KOLD
COAL

BURNS CLEAN

BREAD
ROLLS

CAROLS
BAKERY

CAKES
PIES

OFFICE	OFFICE	SHIPPING RECEIVING
Office	Office	OFFICE
SHIPPING	SHIPPING	SHIPPING RECEIVING
Shipping	Shipping	EMPLOYEES ONLY
RECEIVING	RECEIVING	
Receiving	Receiving	
NO SMOKING	NO SMOKING	

Bigg Industries

Rippoffs General Store
GROCERIES DRUGS SODA HOUSEWARES

TERM OIL CO.

Sparks Electronics
Sales • Repairs • New & Used

APPENDIX B: SUPPLIERS AND MANUFACTURERS

AM Models
Division of Tomar
9520 E. Napier Ave.
Benton Harbor, MI 49022

Bachmann Industries
(Plasticville)
1400 E. Erie Ave.
Philadelphia, PA 19124

Buildings Unlimited
Box 239
Nazareth, PA 18064-0239

Design Preservation Models
Box 66
Linn Creek, MO 65052-0066

Evergreen Scale Models
12808 N.E. 125th Way
Kirkland, WA 98034

Floquil-Polly S Corp.
206 Milvan Dr.
Weston, ON M9L 1Z9
Canada

Grandt Line Products
1040B Shary Ct.
Concord, CA 94518

International Hobby Corp.
413 E. Allegheny Ave.
Philadelphia, PA 19134-2322

Korber Models
2 Tidswell Ave.
Medford, NJ 08055

Lionel Trains
50625 Richard W Blvd.
Chesterfield, MI 48051-2493

Plastruct Inc.
1020 S. Wallace Pl.
City of Industry, CA 91748

Rix Products
3747 Hogue Rd.
Evansville, IN 47712

Wm. K. Walthers Inc.
5601 W. Florist Ave.
Milwaukee, WI 53201-3039